MW01612171

TEN 10-MINUTE SCENES FOR TEENS

By
JENNIFER KIRKEBY

Dramatic Publishing
Woodstock, Illinois • Australia • New Zealand • South Africa

*** NOTICE ***

IMPORTANT BILLING AND CREDIT REQUIREMENTS

All producers of the play must give credit to the author of the play in all programs distributed in connection with performances of the play and in all instances in which the title of the play appears for purposes of advertising, publicizing or otherwise exploiting the play and/or a production. The name of the author must also appear on a separate line, on which no other name appears, immediately following the title, and must appear in size of type not less than fifty percent (50%) the size of the title type. Biographical information on the author, if included in the playbook, may be used in all programs. *In all programs this notice must appear:*

"Produced by special arrangement with
THE DRAMATIC PUBLISHING COMPANY of Woodstock, Illinois"

TEN 10-MINUTE SCENES FOR TEENS

THE COMEDIES

THE DRAMAS

THE COMEDIES

The Elevator

A girl tries to overcome her fear of elevators by riding one for the first time in public.

CHARACTERS:

EMMA. . . . . Terrified of elevators.

JEREMY WALLACE . . Emma's psychiatrist who secretly rides the elevator with her for support.

DARREN . Full of himself. Flirt. In a hurry to get to work.

BRITNEY . . . . Dancer. Friend of Sheila.

SHEILA . . . . Dancer. Friend of Britney.

MARION ALICE MILLER . . . . . An old lady who uses a walker. Hard of hearing.

JIM . . . . Overly friendly inspirational speaker. Wears cowboy hat. Has loud southern drawl.

* * * *

SETTING: *"Out of Order" sign is next to the "elevator." Cheesy elevator music optional.*

AT RISE: *JEREMY enters and walks center stage to elevator. He presses outside button, gets in, holds door open and looks around.*

DARREN *(enters and walks quickly to elevator).* Hold the elevator!

JEREMY. Got it!

DARREN *(gets in elevator).* Thanks, man. I'm going to eleven.

JEREMY. Okay. *(Presses button, but continues holding door open. Looks out.)* I'm holding the door though. I see a few more people coming.

DARREN. Fine. As long as I'm not late to work.

(SHEILA and BRITNEY rush on talking. They are wearing leotards and sweats and carry large bags.)

SHEILA. Hold, please!

DARREN *(sees GIRLS).* You got it! *(To JEREMY.)* Now they're worth waiting for.

BRITNEY *(gets into elevator).* Thanks! The other elevator's out of order.

SHEILA. Can you believe it?

DARREN *(flirting lamely).* No, but my name's Darren, and you can believe that.

BRITNEY & SHEILA *(look at each other and laugh. To JEREMY).* Nine please.

JEREMY. Nine it is! *(Presses button, but continues holding door open.)*

BRITNEY. Thanks. *(She smiles at JEREMY.)*

JEREMY *(looks out).* Here come two more.

DARREN *(to GIRLS).* I'm guessing you're dancers.

BRITNEY & SHEILA. Yeah.
DARREN. Nice.

(EMMA walks nervously toward elevator.)

EMMA. PLEASE HOLD THE ELEVATOR DOORS
  OPEN!
JEREMY. Holding!

*(During the following, EMMA continues walking toward
elevator. She breathes deeply, turns away then turns
back, tries yoga—whatever it takes for her to get to the
elevator. Others [except JEREMY] don't notice her until
she is about to enter the elevator.)*

DARREN *(to GIRLS)*. So, what kind of dancers?
SHEILA. Modern.
DARREN. Cool. I love dancers. Modern or old. I mean
  style-wise. Not old dancers.

(BRITNEY and SHEILA giggle. JEREMY rolls his eyes.)

DARREN *(cont'd., takes photo of GIRLS with his phone)*.
  Now if I could have your numbers to go with this pic-
  ture…
SHEILA *(takes his phone, deletes photo)*. You know,
  Darren. Your pick-up skills leave a lot to be desired.
  (She hands phone back to him.)
DARREN. Well, I've got nine more floors to work on
  some new ones. *(He winks at GIRLS.)*
BRITNEY. Oh, please.

(MARION enters using a walker. She moves toward elevator. EMMA tries to get into elevator. She puts one foot in, takes it out, etc. Everyone is now watching her. She covers her eyes and tries to back into the elevator, but she can't.)

DARREN *(watching EMMA)*. What is she—?

SHEILA *(to EMMA)*. Are you okay?

EMMA *(still covering her eyes)*. I'm scared to ride elevators. Dr. Wallace said that I'm ready to try, though. I want to go all the way to the top, but I just can't seem to...

DARREN. Here. I'll help. *(He picks EMMA up from behind, and then carries her into elevator.)*

EMMA. Hey! Wait!

(Ad libs as DARREN carries her into elevator. Quick and staggered:)

JEREMY. Don't do that!

SHEILA. Leave her alone!

BRITNEY. Put her down!

DARREN *(puts EMMA down in elevator)*. There you go! Easy!

(EMMA stands stunned for a moment. Takes a paper bag out of her purse and begins to breathe into it.)

JEREMY *(still holding door open. To EMMA)*. Are you all right? *(EMMA nods.)*

SHEILA *(to DARREN)*. You could have given her a heart attack!

MARION *(almost at elevator, speaks very loudly)*. Hold the elevator, kids!

DARREN *(sees MARION)*. Speaking of heart attacks… Man, this day just gets better and better!

MARION. Floor eight, please. Going to see if I need hearing aids!

DARREN. Could have saved her a trip…

(JEREMY steps out of elevator and helps MARION enter.)

MARION. Thank you, young man! My, aren't you a nice-looking fellow?

JEREMY. Thank you. Here you go. *(They are now in elevator.)*

JIM *(runs to elevator)*. Hold on there, bronco! *(Notices the crowd. To DARREN.)* Whoa! Is there room in there, cowboy?

(Quick and overlapped:)

DARREN. No!

SHEILA. We're pretty full.

BRITNEY. I don't think there's room for—

JIM *(pushes his way in)*. Thanks kindly! Going up to eleven. Well, isn't this a handsome group! *(He takes off his hat.)* Ladies. I'm Jim. I'm what you call a motivational speaker. Going up to give a seminar right now! Why don't we go around and introduce ourselves?

(EMMA wipes all the elevator keys with an antibacterial wipe. No one else notices.)

DARREN *(to JIM)*. You've got to be kidding me.

(ALL lurch slightly as elevator begins to move.)

EMMA. AAAH! *(Sits down and breathes into her bag.)*

JEREMY *(to EMMA)*. It's okay. It just lurches a little when the elevator moves.

(ALL lurch slightly as elevator stops at floor 2.)

EMMA *(to JEREMY)*. A little? *(Resumes breathing into her bag.)*

DARREN *(announces)*. Second floor. *(Notices buttons.)* Hey! Who pressed all the buttons?

(ALL look at EMMA.)

EMMA. This way it won't go too fast and we'll all be safer. *(She looks around at group.)* Please don't be mad at me. I couldn't stand it if you all got mad at me. *(She is about to cry.)*

(DARREN presses "close door" button which he will continue to do each time. ALL lurch slightly as elevator begins to move.)

JIM *(takes EMMA's hand and helps her up)*. What's your name, darlin'?

EMMA. Emma. *(After she gets up she uses hand sanitizer or a wipe.)*

JIM. Well, Emma. Nobody's mad at you! Heck, we're proud of you! It takes a lot of courage to overcome your fears. That's the first step in my ten-step program! Y'all need to come to one of my seminars. My clients say it's a miracle how much better they feel! *(Hands EMMA his card.)* My card.

DARREN. What's going to be a miracle is if we ever get to our floors. *(ALL lurch slightly as elevator stops on floor 3.)* Floor three. *(He presses button. ALL lurch as elevator begins to move.)*

JIM *(to MARION. Loudly)*. What's your name, young lady?

MARION *(flattered)*. I'm Marion Alice Miller. My maiden name was Clark. In my day we always took our husband's last name. I suppose since he's dead now I could—

(ALL lurch slightly as elevator stops on floor 4.)

DARREN. Fourth floor, people!

JIM *(to MARION)*. Pleasure's all mine, Marion Alice Miller! My card. *(Hands her his card. To BRITNEY and SHEILA.)* Don't believe I caught your names yet. *(Hands them his card.)*

(DARREN presses button. ALL lurch slightly as elevator begins to move.)

BRITNEY. I'm Britney.

SHEILA. I'm Sheila.

JIM. Mighty nice to meet such lovely ladies!

(ALL lurch as elevator stops on floor 5.)

DARREN. Fifth floor. Going once, going twice…

MARION. Sold! *(Starts to exit.)*

JEREMY *(holds door open. Loudly)*. Marion? Didn't you say your doctor was on the eighth floor?

MARION. Yes. Going to find out if I need hearing aids!

JEREMY *(loudly)*. Marion, this isn't your floor. *(He helps her back in.)*

MARION. But it feels like I've been on this elevator for days!

JIM *(offers JEREMY his hand)*. Jim Olson.

JEREMY *(shakes his hand)*. Jeremy.

JIM. Nice to meet you, Jeremy. Here you go! *(Hands JEREMY his card.)*

DARREN *(still holding door open)*. Are we all finally ready? *(OTHERS ignore him. He presses button multiple times.)*

(ALL lurch slightly as elevator begins moving again.)

BRITNEY *(to SHEILA)*. We aren't going to be warmed up at all.

SHEILA. Let's do some *relevés*. *(To MARION. Loudly.)* Do you mind if we hold on to your walker for a bit?

(ALL lurch slightly as elevator stops on floor 6.)

DARREN. Floor six. Pick up sticks.

MARION *(to SHEILA)*. My, you are certainly young to need a walker. But I can understand needing one after all of this standing around!

SHEILA. Thank you.

(DARREN presses button. ALL lurch slightly as elevator begins moving. SHEILA and BRITNEY hold on to the walker and do relevés *and* pliés. *Others, especially DARREN, watch them with interest.)*

JIM *(watching BRITNEY and SHEILA)*. Now that's what I call a good use of time. As my second step clearly states, it's all in your attitude, people. All in your attitude.

(ALL lurch as elevator stops on floor 7.)

DARREN *(stares at BRITNEY and SHEILA)*. Floor seven. I'm in heaven.
EMMA *(to BRITNEY and SHEILA)*. I always wanted to be a dancer.
BRITNEY. Really? Well, you should take some classes.

(DARREN presses button. ALL lurch slightly as elevator begins moving.)

SHEILA. The studio on the ninth floor is really good. And they have beginning classes too. But you'd have to…
EMMA *(smiles)*. I know. Ride the elevator. Maybe someday.

(ALL lurch as elevator stops on floor 8.)

DARREN. Eighth floor!
MARION. Is this my…?
JEREMY. Yes, Marion. This is your floor.

MARION. Thank you! It was very nice meeting you all! Oh, and Emma? You're a very brave girl. Just keep at it, and don't let your fears win, all right?

EMMA. All right. Thank you, Marion!

JEREMY. You have a lovely day, Marion!

MARION. You too, thank you! *(She exits.)*

(DARREN presses button. ALL lurch slightly as elevator begins moving.)

EMMA. Marion sure is a nice lady.

JIM *(begins vocal warm-ups).* HA-HA-HA. BA-BA-BA. TA-TA-TA. GA-GA-GA.

(OTHERS—except DARREN—are amused. ALL lurch as elevator stops on floor 9.)

DARREN. Ninth floor. Goodbye, girls. And remember, I'm only two floors above you if you'd like to come and visit!

SHEILA. Good to know. *(She laughs and gets out of elevator.)*

BRITNEY. Bye, all. Oh, Emma? I hope we see you at the studio sometime, okay?

EMMA. I'll do my best!

(ALL say goodbyes. SHEILA and BRITNEY exit ad libbing. DARREN presses button. ALL lurch slightly as elevator begins moving.)

JIM *(continues his warm-ups).* DA-GA-DA. DA-GA-DA. DA-GA-DA. DA-GA...

DARREN. Seriously? I feel like I'm in *One Flew Over the Cuckoo's Nest*! Cut that out!

JIM. These are vocal warm-ups. Designed to help open the throat and connect the breath. I'll be teaching them at my seminar today.

(ALL lurch as elevator stops on floor 10.)

DARREN. Well, I'm sure sorry I'm going to miss that! *(Laughs.)* Tenth floor, anyone?

JIM. Going to eleven, Darren. HA-HA-HA. BA-BA-BA. *(He continues.)*

(DARREN presses button. ALL lurch slightly as elevator begins moving.)

DARREN *(imitating JIM)*. BLAH-BLAH-BLAH! BLAH-BLAH-BLAH! *(Realizes. To JIM.)* Hey, wait a second. Where are you doing this seminar of yours?

(ALL lurch as elevator stops on floor 11. JEREMY holds door open.)

JIM. Ralph's Refrigeration, my friend.

DARREN *(realizes)*. Oh my god.

JIM. The president of the company told me they've got some real slackers who haven't been doing their jobs. After my all-day motivational seminar, that should change in a hurry! Otherwise, I hear there will be a lot of firing! *(Walks out of elevator. DARREN walks out of elevator with his head down. JIM puts his arm around DARREN.)* So, Darren, do you mind showing me to your office?

(DARREN points.) Let's go get 'em, tiger! *(To EMMA and JEREMY.)* It's been a pleasure meeting you both!

EMMA & JEREMY. You too! Bye! / Bye! *(They laugh as (JIM and DARREN exit.)*

JEREMY. Twelfth floor?

EMMA. Sure.

(JEREMY pushes button. They lurch as elevator begins to move. They stare silently up at the lights indicating the floors. They lurch again as elevator stops on floor 12. Once they've stopped, JEREMY holds door open, looks out and sees no one is around.)

EMMA *(smiles)*. I did it!

JEREMY. Yes, you did!

EMMA. You know, seeing how strange people like Darren and Jim are actually made me feel like I'm not so weird after all.

JEREMY *(laughs)*. It was an interesting group, that's for sure. Well, what would you like to do? I can't hold this door much longer. And what goes up must come down.

EMMA *(takes a deep breath)*. Let's go back down.

JEREMY. Okay! *(He presses button.)*

(Doors close. They lurch as elevator begins to go down.)

EMMA. Thanks for being with me today, Dr. Wallace. It really helped!

JEREMY. I wouldn't have missed it for the world, Emma.

BLACKOUT

Ghost Trackers

Four high school students visit a haunted house in the hopes of catching paranormal activity for a school project.

CHARACTERS:

SABRINA . . . . Directs the film. She takes the project very seriously.

MATT. . . . . Co-host of the project. His acting skills leave much to be desired.

VINNIE. . . . . Cameraman and class clown.

AMBER . . . . . . Co-host of the project. Very good at what she does. She gets frustrated with Matt.

GHOST OF MRS. PEABODY . . . . A woman who died in the house 50 years ago. She wears a long black dress. There is a rope around her neck.

* * * *

AT RISE: *VINNIE runs onstage wearing a backpack. He opens "front door" and enters house.*

VINNIE. This is so awesome, you guys! A real haunted house! Hurry up! You've got to see this!

(SABRINA enters carrying a bag. She looks around. AMBER enters with her.)

SABRINA. Wow! It's perfect!
AMBER. No kidding! *(Looking behind her, she calls out.)* Matt, where are you?
VINNIE. Shhh. I'm going to scare him. *(He exits to hide.)*

(Loud thumping offstage.)

MATT. Owww! *(He calls out.)* I tripped on the front step!
SABRINA *(to MATT)*. Are you all right?
MATT. Yeah. *(He enters adjusting his bag. He looks around room.)* Whoa, this is cool!
SABRINA. Close the door, Matt. *(He does.)* Let's put our bags over here. *(They do.)*
AMBER. We're so lucky to get to use this house for the night.
MATT. Where's Vinnie?
AMBER. He's—

(VINNIE enters with his arms straight out. He's zipped up his jacket with his head hidden inside.)

VINNIE. Ooooo! Someone cut off my head, and you're next, Matt! *(He walks toward MATT.)*
MATT. Seriously, Vinnie?

VINNIE *(as a ghost)*. I'm not Vinnie. I'm the ghost of Mrs. Peabody! I have come back to reclaim my house! Ooooo!

SABRINA. That's enough, Vinnie. We've got a lot to do. *(She opens her bag and takes out her iPod and portable speaker deck.)*

VINNIE *(unzips his jacket)*. Fine. You have to admit you were a little scared though. Right, Matt?

MATT *(sarcastically)*. Terrified.

VINNIE *(gets his video camera from backpack)*. It's not a coincidence that Vincent van Gogh and I share the same name. He wasn't appreciated in his lifetime either.

AMBER. Vinnie, you're only seventeen. There's still hope.

SABRINA. Can we please run through the opening?

MATT. Sure.

AMBER. Who's got the microphones?

VINNIE. I do. *(He gets two wireless microphones and hands them to AMBER and MATT.)*

SABRINA *(looks around room)*. Let's start with Amber and Matt standing by the entrance. What do you think, Vinnie?

VINNIE. Works for me! *(To AMBER and MATT.)* You guys ready?

AMBER & MATT. Ready!

SABRINA. Great. All right, everyone. From the intro. *(She stands near VINNIE, holds up five fingers and counts them down:)* Five, four, three, two, one, *(points at AMBER and MATT)* action!

AMBER. Amber Danielle here with Matt Jackson, and we are…

AMBER & MATT. The Ghost Trackers!

AMBER. Tonight we are inside Mrs. Peabody's mansion. There have been numerous documented ghost sightings in this house. Tonight we will try to find out if the stories are true—that Mrs. Peabody still haunts her house fifty years after she hung herself in this very room.

MATT *(painfully overacted)*. That's right, Amber! After discovering her husband and their longtime housekeeper were having an affair, Mrs. Peabody called them into this room on that fateful night and hung herself before their very eyes!

SABRINA. Cut!

MATT. Bad lighting?

VINNIE. The lighting isn't what's bad, dude.

SABRINA. Vinnie, I'm the director. Uh, Matt?

MATT. Yeah?

SABRINA. Can you make your delivery a little more... natural?

MATT. Natural?

SABRINA. Yeah, you know—like you're just talking to a friend. Not selling an energy drink.

MATT. I was just trying to be enthusiastic.

SABRINA. Enthusiasm is great, Matt. Just keep it real.

MATT. Got it.

SABRINA. Thanks. Oh, and can you both walk across the room during the intro? I'd like to capture more of the space. Let's take it from your section, Matt. Here we go! *(She holds up five fingers and counts them down:)* Five, four, three, two, one, *(points at MATT)* action!

MATT *(overly serious and too quiet)*. That's right, Amber. After discovering her husband and their longtime housekeeper were having an affair, Mrs. Peabody called them into this room on that fateful night and hung herself before their very eyes.

SABRINA. Cut! Matt, what are you doing?

MATT. This is how I talk to my friends, Sabrina.

AMBER. No you don't!

VINNIE. Wait, you have friends?

MATT. Only cool ones. That's why you're not one of them, Vinnie.

SABRINA *(exhales)*. Matt, now no one is going to hear you. And if they do, they aren't going to care! This has to be exciting and mysterious, but also believable.

MATT. I'm getting mixed signals here, Sabrina.

SABRINA. Like that! Hear how you just talked to me? It was natural, but passionate.

MATT. Okay. I'll try.

VINNIE. Good thing we have all night.

MATT. Shut it, van Gogh.

SABRINA. That's enough, guys. Let's do this. Matt, just find a happy medium.

VINNIE *(laughs)*. Good one! A happy medium, get it? *(No one responds.)* Medium? Like a psychic? *(Looks at OTHERS.)* Nothing? Fine. *(Gets ready to film.)*

SABRINA *(trying to stay positive)*. All right, everyone! Third time's a charm! From Matt's intro! *(She holds up five fingers and counts them down:)* Five, four, three, two, one, *(points at MATT)* action!

MATT *(begins "over the top," but settles into being believable)*. That's right, Amber! After discovering her husband and their longtime housekeeper were having an affair, Mrs. Peabody called them into this room on that fateful night, and hung herself before their very eyes! *(He looks at SABRINA for guidance.)*

(SABRINA gives MATT a "thumbs-up." Everyone is relieved.)

AMBER. Many people believe that Mrs. Peabody's ghost returned for revenge. Within a week of her suicide, her husband had a heart attack and the housekeeper mysteriously fell down those stairs to her death. *(She points to "stairs")*

MATT. We've brought our team of expert Ghost Trackers with us tonight to try and communicate with the spirit of Mrs. Peabody. But for that job, I'm going to get a very special machine, the Ghost Tracker! *(He runs to his bag and gets machine.)*

AMBER. As I mentioned previously, many ghost sightings have been documented in and around this house. Some people have seen a woman in a long black dress floating down the halls. Others have heard footsteps and moaning sounds. We believe the ghost of Mrs. Peabody still occupies this house. And tonight we hope to prove it.

MATT. We sure do, Amber. Let's turn on our official Ghost Tracker and see what we pick up.

(As MATT turns on Ghost Tracker, SABRINA turns on her iPod which plays sound effects for the Ghost Tracker machine. MATT and AMBER walk around the room as if tracking ghosts as:)

AMBER. Our custom-made Ghost Tracker can pick up signals that no other machine can. Its highly sensitive features will recognize and record any paranormal activity. *(SABRINA knocks on floor. AMBER gasps.)* Did you hear that, Matt?

MATT. Yes Amber, I did!

(SABRINA knocks on floor.)

AMBER *(gasps)*. There it is again! It sounds like some sort of knocking!

MATT *(adjusts the Ghost Tracker)*. It's probably Mrs. Peabody trying to communicate with us!

AMBER *(shivers)*. Oh my gosh. I just felt cold chills going up my back! *(Shivers.)* It happened again! Did you feel anything, Matt?

MATT *(not sure if AMBER is acting)*. Seriously?

AMBER *(frustrated with MATT, but tries to get him to catch on)*. Yes, Matt! Seriously. Whoa! Now I feel like my energy is draining! Check the Ghost Tracker for activity. I'm definitely sensing something very powerful!

MATT. You are? *(He looks at machine.)* It's moving, Amber! The numbers are going up!

AMBER. Really? *(She looks at machine and is genuinely surprised. She looks at SABRINA who motions for them to continue. AMBER calls out.)* Mrs. Peabody? Is that you? *(Beat.)* Can you send us a sign?

MATT *(calls out)*. You're probably mad at your husband and housekeeper, and we don't blame you!

(SABRINA turns on the following sound effects: a creaking door opening, howling wind, door slamming shut.)

MATT *(cont'd)*. Did you hear that, Amber?

AMBER. Yes, Matt. I did.

MATT *(breaks character and looks at SABRINA).* Okay, seriously. Was that you, Sabrina?

SABRINA. Cut!

VINNIE *(puts down camera).* Oh good. I've got to find a bathroom. I drank three Red Bulls on the way over here. *(He runs offstage.)*

SABRINA. Matt, we talked about the sound effects that I'd be playing on my iPod during this. Don't break character in the middle of a scene!

MATT. But how did you make the numbers move on the Ghost Tracker?

AMBER. They really did, Sabrina.

SABRINA. Let me see. *(MATT and AMBER bring machine to her.)* It's just some old machine I found. It probably has a little juice left in it. *(They all look at machine.)* Whoa. It is moving!

(Ghost-like moaning is heard from offstage.)

MATT. Is that your iPod?

SABRINA. No. I...I'm sure it's just Vinnie playing around. *(Calls out.)* Vinnie! Cut it out!

(Ghost-like moaning is heard from offstage.)

AMBER *(calls out).* Stop it, Vinnie!

MATT. Vinnie! You're scaring the girls! *(AMBER and SABRINA shoot him a look.)* And me!

(Thunder sound effects. Lights go out. KIDS yell or scream.)

SABRINA. Don't move. I brought flashlights.

(She takes out three flashlights from her bag and hands one each to AMBER and MATT. They turn on flashlights and shine the light around the room.)

AMBER *(calls out)*. Vinnie, if you turned off the lights, I'm going to kill you!

MATT. Not if I get to him first!

SABRINA. Shh. Stay calm you guys. It could just be a blown circuit. Happens all the time at my house.

(Louder ghost-like moaning is heard.)

AMBER *(terrified)*. What is that?

SABRINA *(calls out)*. Vinnie! Get back here! *(To AMBER and MATT.)* Get your stuff.

AMBER. We can't leave Vinnie!

MATT. Watch me. *(Calls out.)* Vinnie! This is seriously your last chance! We are leaving!

SABRINA. Our bags are over here. *(They move to bags staying close together.)*

VINNIE *(jumps into their light and yells)*. BOO!

(KIDS scream or yell.)

MATT. Vinnie, you idiot! *(He shoves VINNIE to ground.)*

VINNIE *(stands)*. Hey! Not cool, bro!

AMBER. Neither is scaring us to death. Did you turn the lights off?

VINNIE. No. But I sure got lost in the dark. I think I walked through the entire house!

SABRINA. Didn't you hear us yelling for you?

VINNIE. No, I really didn't. This house is like sound-proofed or something.

SABRINA. Well, we're leaving. *(She hands VINNIE a flashlight.)* Come on!

(Louder ghost-like moaning from offstage.)

VINNIE. Dude! What was that?

(Following sound effects begin in quick succession: Ghost moaning, footsteps, chains being dragged, evil laughter, doors opening and closing, thunder, howling wind, screams, cat screeching, etc. Lightning effects can also be used. KIDS run to the front door. Following dialogue is overlapped and fast.)

MATT. We've got to get out of here!

AMBER. Oh my god! Somebody help!

SABRINA. Hurry up, you guys!

VINNIE. Go, go, go, go, go!!!

(When they get to the "front door" MATT tries to open it. It's locked. They all struggle to try and open it. They ad lib reactions. Sound effects continue.

In the meantime, the GHOST OF MRS. PEABODY has entered from another part of the stage. She is filming the KIDS with a video camera. She moans loudly. Then silence.

KIDS stop struggling with the door and turn slowly toward her with their flashlights. They yell and then freeze with terror.

GHOST continues filming KIDS. She turns to audience.)

GHOST OF MRS. PEABODY. This is going to go viral! *(She turns back to KIDS and continues filming.)*

BLACKOUT

Prom Royalty was first produced by FAIR School Downtown. It premiered January 12, 2012, at the New Century Theatre City Center in Minneapolis, Minn., with the following:

CAST

CLAIRE . . . . Megan Johnson
SHANIA . . . . Alexa Pearson
JEFF . . . . Forest Rys-Fitch
VINCENT . . . . Max Singer

PRODUCTION STAFF & CREW

Artistic Director . . . . Sandy Boren-Barrett
Director . . . . Adam Hegg
Set/Props Designer . . . . Jim Hibbeler
Lighting/Technical Director. . . . . Gretchen Katt
Costume Designer . . . . Shannon O'Black
Stage Manager . . . . Jenny Moeller
Assistant Stage Manager/Production Manager . . . . Melanie
Salmon-Peterson

Prom Royalty

What begins as a wonderful parade ride for high-school royalty dissolves into disaster. Music and SFX optional.

CHARACTERS:

CLAIRE . . Senior prom queen. This is the most important
day of her life. She wants everything to be perfect.
Self-absorbed. Bubbly and upbeat—at first.

SHANIA. . . . . Junior prom princess. Gets tired of Claire's
selfishness. Sarcastic.

JEFF . . . . Senior prom king. Claire's boyfriend.
Feels torn between Claire's expectations
and wanting to have fun.

VINCENT . . . . . . Junior prom prince. Shania's boyfriend.
Class clown and proud of it.

* * * *

AT RISE: *CLAIRE, SHANIA, JEFF and VINCENT are sitting in chairs, possibly on some sort of platform that is the "float." Two could sit in chairs and two behind could sit on higher stools. During the scene they are smiling and waving at the "people" they are passing. They occasionally throw "candy" at the crowd.*

They continue to smile and wave for a while in silence. Eventually, CLAIRE can no longer contain herself.)

CLAIRE. This is the best day of my life! I have dreamt of being prom queen forever! Look at all these people staring at us! Shania, is my hair holding curl?

SHANIA. Yes, Claire. It looks great. What about mine?

CLAIRE. What about your what?

SHANIA. My hair, Claire. How's my hair?

CLAIRE *(glances at SHANIA's hair)*. It looks fine. Is my crown straight? Jeff, smile!

JEFF. I am smiling. It's not easy to smile this long.

CLAIRE. We've only gone four blocks!

JEFF. You're kidding.

CLAIRE. I would never kid about our responsibilities as royals.

VINCENT. Royal pains in the a—

(BOYS laugh.)

SHANIA *(interrupts)*. Vincent! You promised to take this seriously! After all, the school voted us prom princess and prince.

CLAIRE. Junior.

SHANIA. Excuse me?

CLAIRE. They voted you junior prom princess and prince.

SHANIA. Well, yeah. That's because we're juniors.

CLAIRE. Right. And Jeff and I are senior prom queen and king.

SHANIA. Right. Because you're seniors.

CLAIRE. Exactly! Shania?

SHANIA. What?

CLAIRE. My crown?

SHANIA. What about it?

CLAIRE. Is it straight?

SHANIA. Yes, Claire. Your crown is straight. Trust me, with all the hair spray you used, you'll need a chisel to get it off your head.

CLAIRE *(ignores remark)*. We'll need to keep checking each other to be sure we look our best. _____ *(Insert popular local TV station.)* is going to be here! _____ *(Insert popular woman anchor.)* is my idol! I want to be just like her when I get old!

(VINCENT has taken out his cell phone and is texting with one hand and waving with the other. JEFF takes out his phone and begins texting VINCENT. He also continues waving.)

SHANIA. She's not old.

CLAIRE. Well, she is compared to us. *(She looks to stage right.)* Awww. Look at those cute kids! Boys! Stage right! Candy toss! *(VINCENT and JEFF throw "candy" left but continue looking at their phones.)* You guys! That was stage left!

VINCENT. What are you talking about?

SHANIA *(a bit sarcastically)*. Don't you remember, Vincent? Claire gave us stage directions so we'd know which side of the street to look, where to throw candy, and where the news cameras are.

CLAIRE. Those kids didn't get any candy! *(Notices BOYS are texting. She gasps.)* You've got to be kidding me! You're texting? On the most important day of our lives?!

VINCENT. The most important day of your life...

CLAIRE. No way! Give me those phones.

JEFF. We'll put them away. *(He puts phone in his pocket.)*

CLAIRE *(tries to get JEFF's phone while continuing to wave and smile).* Give me, give me, give me!

JEFF. Chill, Claire!

VINCENT *(puts phone in pocket).* It was an emergency.

CLAIRE. Oh, really? What emergency could possibly take precedence over your royal responsibilities?

VINCENT. It's uh...my grandmother.

JEFF. Yeah, my grandmother. I mean, Vincent's grandmother.

CLAIRE. Is she sick?

VINCENT.	JEFF.
No.	Yes.
Yes.	No.

SHANIA. Wow. How original.

CLAIRE. Give me a break, you guys! How would you feel if your grandmother really was—

SHANIA. Stage left! Candy toss!

(BOYS throw candy to their right.)

CLAIRE. Seriously? That was stage right! You need to pay attention. Jeff! What kind of a senior prom king are you being? You missed the kids again!

(BOYS turn and throw candy hard to their left.)

JEFF. Got 'em!

VINCENT. Whoa! We sure did! *(BOYS laugh.)*

CLAIRE *(takes a deep breath trying to stay calm).* All right. Did you boys hear me when I said _____ *(Insert local news station.)* is in the crowd? We are going to be on the news! Think of the publicity!

SHANIA. Yeah, you guys. *(She looks front and is repulsed.)* Ewww. I just wish we didn't end up behind horses. That is so disgusting.

(They all look. BOYS begin laughing.)

VINCENT. Dude! That is totally gross!

JEFF. Whoa, look at all that horse sh— *(or "crap.")*

CLAIRE *(interrupts).* Jeff!

VINCENT. What do those things eat anyway? *(He takes out his cell phone and takes a picture.)*

CLAIRE. Oh. My. Gosh. You are so disgusting! May I remind you that we were told specifically not to look at the horses when they—

SHANIA. Stage right! Candy toss! *(BOYS throw candy to their right.)* Good job!

JEFF. Thanks, Shania.

CLAIRE. Finally.

(VINCENT shows picture to JEFF. They react.)

JEFF. Dude, I would not eat candy that was on this rode!

CLAIRE *(angry, but continues to smile and wave).* Put your phone away, Vincent!

SHANIA. That's enough, you guys. Seriously. You're supposed to be role models.

JEFF & VINCENT. Sorry. *(VINCENT puts phone away.)*

CLAIRE. Thank you, Vincent.

VINCENT. You bet.

JEFF. Mr. Hoskins ahead.

CLAIRE. Stage right or stage left?

JEFF. I don't know. He's on your left.

CLAIRE. Well, Jeff. That would be stage left!

JEFF. Then why don't you just say left?

ALL *(beaming except for VINCENT who isn't smiling)*. Hi Mr. Hoskins!

SHANIA. What grade did he give you, Vincent?

VINCENT. Let's not ruin this special day. *(He notices a cute girl to his right. He tries to get JEFF's attention, but can't. He takes a photo and texts it to JEFF.)*

JEFF *(takes out his phone and looks at photo)*. Nice!

CLAIRE. What is it?

JEFF. Nothing!

(CLAIRE grabs JEFF's phone and sees picture. She is furious. She keeps his phone and then waves so hard that she hits JEFF.)

JEFF *(cont'd)*. Owww! Why'd you do that?

CLAIRE. Because you took a picture of Sylvia!

JEFF. No I didn't! Vincent did!

(SHANIA waves hard and hits VINCENT.)

VINCENT *(to SHANIA)*. Seriously?

SHANIA. Very. Candy, stage right!

(BOYS throw candy to left. ALL lurch forward.)

SHANIA *(cont'd)*. Really, you guys? Sylvia? How original. Every guy in the school has—
CLAIRE. Shhh! Shania! She's right there. And the float's stopped.
SHANIA. I don't care!
CLAIRE. Don't panic. Just look stage left and keep waving!

(GIRLS look left, smile and continue waving.)

SHANIA. No one's panicking, Claire!

(BOYS are looking at SYLVIA right. They toss her candy.)

CLAIRE *(to BOYS)*. I said, look stage left!

(BOYS look left, but sneak looks at SYLVIA.)

SHANIA *(looks right)*. Oh, crap. Claire? Sylvia's waving at us. What should we do?
CLAIRE. Please do not say that disgusting word next to my name! Just ignore her.
SHANIA. That's kind of hard. She's waving right at us.
CLAIRE *(accusing BOYS)*. Are you sure she's looking at us? Just don't look at her!
SHANIA. It's too late! She just said "hi" to us!
CLAIRE. Oh, fine. On my count: 1, 2, 3…
GIRLS *(big smiles)*. Hi, Sylvia!
VINCENT. Hypocrites.

SHANIA. Really, Vincent? Really?

VINCENT. Well, yeah. I mean we're not even allowed to look at her.

SHANIA. There is a big difference between looking and drooling all over yourself.

VINCENT. I wasn't drooling! Jeff, were you drooling again?

(ALL lurch back. Float has begun moving again.)

CLAIRE. Oh good. We're moving again. All I can say is that I expect more from my fellow royals. Especially my boyfriend.

JEFF. Claire, don't be mad.

CLAIRE. I wouldn't be mad if you'd start being respectful to your title, your school and your public! How hard is it just to smile and wave?

JEFF. Depends on how long you have to do it.

VINCENT. That's what she said.

(KIDS—except CLAIRE—crack up. BOYS high-five each other and go back to waving.)

CLAIRE *(seething)*. I am very close to my breaking point. Shall I go over our promises to our school? Shall remind you about indecent, inappropriate and obscene behavior, and how it is not tolerated by royalty? Do you want to lose your titles?

BOYS. No.

SHANIA. Candy toss.

(JEFF tosses candy right. VINCENT tosses candy to left. Some candy hits CLAIRE's head.)

CLAIRE. Owww! GIVE ME THE DAMN CANDY!

(They give her candy. Silence for a while. OTHERS try not to laugh.)

JEFF *(tries to make up)*. You sure look beautiful, Claire. *(CLAIRE ignores him.)* Your eyes are sparkly like your crown.
VINCENT. They really are, Claire. Sparkly.
SHANIA. Shut up, Vincent.

(CLAIRE ignores them. She is trying not to cry.)

JEFF. Claire?
SHANIA. Oh no. Is that rain?
CLAIRE. No! My hair! *(She begins to cry.)*

(JEFF tries to shield CLAIRE from the rain. He accidentally knocks her crown off onto the road.)

CLAIRE *(cont'd)*. MY CROWN!

(JEFF tries to reach it, but falls over onto CLAIRE. CLAIRE screams.)

VINCENT. Dude! It fell right into the horse sh— *(Or "crap." He takes a picture of the crown.)*
CLAIRE. YOU IDIOT!

(She pushes JEFF off of her and jumps up to get VIN-CENT's phone. They struggle. SHANIA and JEFF get up to try and separate them.

Following lines are frantic although they try to continue smiling and waving.)

SHANIA. Claire, settle down! Everyone's watching!
JEFF. Claire Bear! Sit down!
VINCENT. Claire Bear?
CLAIRE *(to VINCENT)*. Give me that phone!

(Arguing continues until:)

SHANIA. Oh my god! You guys! It's _____ *(Local TV station.)* and they're filming us!

(They all look out and feebly smile and wave.)

CLAIRE *(wails)*. It's _____! *(Insert popular local female TV anchor. CLAIRE cries.)*
VINCENT *(begins taking video with his phone)*. Dude, this is so awesome! Do you know how many hits this is going to get?
CLAIRE. NOT AS MANY AS YOU!

(CLAIRE frantically tries to get VINCENT's phone. They all yell and try to pull CLAIRE away from VIN-CENT. He holds his camera out and continues taking video.)

BLACKOUT

Subtext

BOY and GIRL on a first date. Their inner thoughts (SUB and TEXT) follow them around and make judgmental comments. BOY and GIRL don't hear SUB and TEXT at first. Eventually, they do.

CHARACTERS:

BOY. . . Boy on a first date. Kind, thoughtful and nervous.

GIRL . . . . Girl on a first date. Insecure and nervous but a nice girl.

SUB (w) . . . . Girl's inner thoughts.

TEXT (m). . . . . Boy's inner thoughts.

* * * *

SETTING: *Onstage there are two chairs. Offstage is a pre-set table for the restaurant.*

AT RISE: *GIRL is getting ready for a date. She is looking in a "mirror" and fixing her hair. She is nervous but tries to pump herself up. SUB is onstage watching GIRL.*

GIRL. Okay, okay. I look pretty good. Better than most. *(She tries a few poses. With a sexy voice she says:)* Hi there. Like what you see?

SUB. Uh, maybe before you turn into Narcissus you should take a closer look into the "mirror mirror on the wall."

GIRL *(moves closer to "mirror" and gasps)*. Oh my god! I have a zit! When did that happen? NO! He'll be here in five minutes. Cover-up! Where's my cover-up? *(She looks around frantically. She can't find it.)* Did I leave it in my car? *(She runs off.)*

(SUB follows GIRL offstage shaking her head. BOY enters holding flowers. TEXT follows BOY.)

BOY *(to himself)*. I hope she likes daisies. Shoot. What if she likes roses better? But roses are for when you're in love, right? This is just a first date. I mean, I like her and everything, but I don't love her. *(Smiles.)* Of course that could change by the end of tonight.

TEXT. Right. She's going to fall in love with you. Over daisies. Please. You have this tiny window of opportunity to show her that you're a classy guy. And you bring her daisies. Fork over the dough, cheapskate, and show the lady that you care.

BOY *(looks at his watch)*. I still have time to get her roses. *(He runs off.)*

(TEXT follows BOY offstage shaking his head. GIRL runs onstage to mirror with cover-up and Kleenex. SUB follows GIRL and watches her.)

GIRL *(looking in mirror)*. Okay. Don't panic. This stuff
works great. He'll never notice.

SUB. Right. He'll never notice that you have a zit the size
of Rhode Island right in the middle of your nose. If
you're lucky he'll be farsighted and will forget his
glasses.

GIRL. Ugh! Who am I kidding! This thing is HUGE! Why
couldn't we get zits on the bottoms of our feet, or
somewhere nobody looks? Life is so unfair! *(Tries to
apply cover-up. She is shaking badly and puts too much
on her face.)* NO! It's everywhere BUT the zit!

SUB. Girl, this is not your night.

GIRL. He'll be here any second! *(She wipes off the
cover-up and looks in mirror.)* Breathe. It will be all
right. Stop being so emotional and get ready!

*(BOY enters holding roses and a box of chocolate.
TEXT enters behind BOY.)*

BOY. I can't believe how much roses cost! And these
chocolates! Man! I'll be lucky if I can still pay for dinner! Hopefully she'll offer to pay half. *(He walks toward GIRL's house. He takes out his phone and double
checks the address.)* It's showtime!

GIRL *(checks herself)*. Okay. That's better. Just need lipstick. *(She begins to put it on. BOY knocks on door or
rings doorbell. The noise scares her and she smears lipstick.)* NO!

BOY. That doesn't sound good...

GIRL *(rushes over to door. Looks through peephole)*.
Awww. He brought roses!

SUB *(behind GIRL)*. You know what that means. He expects more than good conversation.

BOY. I wonder what's up? *(Looks through peephole from other side.)*

TEXT *(behind BOY)*. What's up is she's probably looking at you through the peephole trying to decide whether or not to open the door. Now step back and try to look cool for a change. *(BOY does.)*

GIRL. He is so cool!

SUB. You can tell that from looking through the peephole?

GIRL *(opens door)*. Hi!

BOY. Hi!

(They stand and smile at each other awkwardly.)

TEXT. Dude! Say something! She's obviously nervous. I mean, look at her lipstick! *(He laughs.)*

BOY. I brought you roses. *(He hands them to her.)*

GIRL. My favorite! Thanks so much! *(She takes roses.)*

(They stand and smile at each other awkwardly.)

SUB. Are you going to ask him in, or are you going to stand here like an idiot all night?

GIRL. Come in! I was just finishing up.

BOY. Thanks. *(He enters.)* Oh, I brought you these too. *(Hands her chocolates.)*

SUB. Looks like he's expecting a lot tonight!

GIRL. How sweet! *(Indicating chair.)* Here, have a seat. I'll just be a second.

BOY. Okay. *(He sits in chair.)*

GIRL *(runs offstage with roses and candy. Runs to mirror and sees lipstick smear)*. NO!

BOY *(startled)*. Are you okay?

GIRL *(calls out)*. Yes, I'm fine! *(To herself.)* He must think I'm crazy!

BOY *(to himself)*. Why does she keep yelling no?

TEXT. Three guesses. She doesn't like you, she just noticed her lipstick, or she doesn't like you.

BOY. She probably just noticed her lipstick. *(He and TEXT laugh.)*

GIRL *(calls out)*. Almost ready!

BOY. Okay!

TEXT. It's about time.

GIRL *(walks to BOY)*. I'm so embarrassed. My makeup was a mess when you got here.

BOY. I didn't notice. *(Looks at her.)* You look beautiful.

TEXT. Way to keep her guessing, dude. "You look beautiful"? The next lame thing I expect to hear is her saying how handsome you look.

GIRL. Thanks! You look really handsome.

(SUB and TEXT groan.)

BOY. Thanks. *(Laughs.)*

GIRL. What's funny?

BOY. Nothing. It's just...I don't think anyone's told me that I look handsome except my mom.

TEXT. Already bringing "Mommy" into the conversation and you haven't even left the house. Way to stay cool, dude! *(He laughs.)*

BOY. Not that my mom says it that often, I mean, just when I dress up for a date...or church...or something.

TEXT. Wow. You should write a book on what NOT to say on a first date.

GIRL. I think that's sweet. You must have a very nice mom. *(She gets her purse. They exit the house and begin to walk.)*

SUB. Good save.

BOY. Mom's all right. What kind of food do you like?

GIRL. Anything. What do you like?

SUB. Really? Anything? You're allergic to shellfish, you hate cheeseburgers, and you're not even that hungry. So why don't you tell him that?

BOY *(stops walking)*. I thought we could go to the fish place down the street. Or there's that burger place a block away.

SUB. It's now or never. Tell him!

GIRL. Actually, I'm allergic to shellfish and I don't care for cheeseburgers. But anything else is fine.

SUB. Good girl. It's always best to be honest.

TEXT. Whoa! Do you see the red flashing sign above this girl's head blinking: "High Maintenance! High Maintenance!"? Because I sure do!

BOY. Oh. Well, how about Italian?

GIRL. Perfect!

TEXT. Yeah. Perfect. Nothing like garlic breath to make a girl want to kiss you…

GIRL. Let's go to Giovanni's around the corner.

BOY. Great! Hope you don't mind garlic breath! *(Laughs nervously.)*

GIRL. Hope you don't! *(Laughs nervously.)*

BOY. I don't.

SUB. How would he know that unless he's kissed a lot of girls with garlic breath?

GIRL. Me either.

TEXT. How would she know that unless…

BOY *(he heard TEXT; stops and looks at GIRL)*. Did you hear that?

GIRL. Hear what?

BOY *(looks around)*. Oh, nothing. I just thought— *(Listens.)* It was nothing.

GIRL. Well, here we are!

(BOY and GIRL enter restaurant. SUB and TEXT become their waiters. They bring on pre-set table with a white tablecloth, roses in vase and two chairs.)

SUB *(to BOY and GIRL)*. Welcome to Giovanni's! Table for two?

BOY. Yes please.

SUB. Right this way! *(She leads them to table.)*

(TEXT pulls out GIRL's chair. Once she is seated, he pushes chair in and does the same for BOY. When he is done, he stands with a towel over his bent arm like a fancy waiter.)

SUB *(hands them menus. To GIRL)*. You're right. He is handsome. *(To both.)* Would you like to hear our specials?

GIRL *(shocked. To BOY)*. Did you hear what she said?

BOY. She asked if we'd like to hear the specials. Would you?

GIRL *(still baffled)*. No. No thank you.

SUB. Okay. Well, they're listed on the first page of the menu if you'd like to see them.

GIRL & BOY. Thank you.

SUB. Drinks?

GIRL. I'll have a Diet Coke.

SUB. One Diet Coke. And for you, handsome?

BOY. I'll have the same.

SUB. Coming right up! *(She exits.)*

GIRL *(gasps)*. Did you hear her that time? She called you handsome!

BOY *(smiling)*. Twice in one night!

GIRL. Yes, but—

SUB *(enters with drinks. He puts them on table)*. Here we go! Ready to order?

BOY. Not quite.

SUB. No problem. We'll be right here when you're ready! *(She stands next to TEXT.)*

GIRL *(sips her drink)*. You know those voices inside your head that tell you you're not good enough?

BOY *(takes a gulp of his drink)*. Well...

SUB. Oooo. She's getting all serious before they've even ordered!

TEXT. Yeah. This is going to be one exciting night, I can tell. Yawn.

GIRL *(points at SUB)*. See? Like that! Those are not helpful things to be in my head.

BOY *(unaware)*. The servers?

GIRL. No, not the servers! The smart-aleck remarks that girl keeps saying!

TEXT *(to SUB)*. Oh, snap! She's figured you out!

BOY *(hears TEXT)*. I'm not sure what you—

GIRL. I'm talking about those voices of insecurity we all have. I was so worried about the zit on my nose earlier that I almost had a seizure!

BOY. I didn't even notice…

TEXT. Yeah, right!

BOY *(to TEXT)*. Shut up!

GIRL. Me?

BOY. No, no. *(Points to TEXT.)* Him!

GIRL. So you do know what I'm saying!

BOY. Daisies.

GIRL. What?

BOY. I bought you daisies earlier.

GIRL. How sweet!

BOY. Yeah, but I worried that you wouldn't like them. So I went out and bought roses and chocolate.

GIRL. They're nice too. But I love daisies. *(She smiles at him.)*

BOY. You do?

GIRL. Yes. And I really like you. You're probably the nicest guy that's ever asked me out.

(SUB and TEXT make gagging noises.)

BOY *(to TEXT)*.   GIRL *(to SUB)*.
  Shut up!   Shut up!

TEXT. Oh no.

SUB. Is it going to happen?

TEXT. I think so.

BOY. I've got an idea.

SUB. Here it comes!

GIRL. What's that?

BOY *(looks at TEXT)*. Let's leave these loser voices in the restaurant and we'll get you some daisies. *(Stands up and reaches for GIRL's hand.)*

GIRL. Great idea! *(She takes BOY's hand and stands. She looks at SUB.)* Who needs them? *(They begin to exit. To BOY.)* Oh, can we get some frozen yogurt?

BOY. I love frozen yogurt!

GIRL. Just imagine the fun we'll have without those two blabbing in our ears!

(They laugh as they exit. SUB and TEXT try talking to BOY and GIRL but nothing comes out. They try talking to each other. Silence. They look defeated.)

BLACKOUT

Time Warp

A present-day teenage boy and a fairy-tale princess discover that their lives have magically intersected.

CHARACTERS:

NATHAN . . . . Teenage boy.

BETHANY . . . . A high-maintenance mean girl. Nathan's girlfriend.

PRINCESS ELIZABETH . . . A real princess whose castle and village were just burned down by the dragon.

DRAGON . . . . A dragon who is out to get Princess Elizabeth.

* * * *

AT RISE: *Lights up on NATHAN who is listening to his iPod with headphones and playing air guitar. His eyes are closed. He is in his own world.*

PRINCESS *(runs onstage)*. Help me! Please, help me!

(NATHAN continues playing air guitar. He doesn't see or hear PRINCESS.)

PRINCESS *(cont'd., sees NATHAN)*. Oh, thank heavens! *(She runs to him.)* Won't you help me, kind sir? A dragon has burned down my castle and now he is after me!

(NATHAN begins "playing" a complicated riff. Still with his eyes closed, he moves around and begins to sing the notes loudly.)

PRINCESS *(cont'd)*. Oh dear. It appears that the only survivor besides me is the village idiot. Whatever shall I do? *(She looks offstage.)* The dragon! Someone help me! *(She runs offstage in the other direction.)*

(NATHAN comes downstage as the rock star he imagines himself to be. He sits down, still "playing" and scoots himself backward.

Meanwhile, PRINCESS runs back on and almost trips over NATHAN.)

NATHAN *(sees PRINCESS and jumps up)*. Whoa!

PRINCESS. So now you see me?

NATHAN *(shocked and somewhat embarrassed. He takes off headphones)*. I'm sorry?

PRINCESS. And well you should be ignoring a damsel in distress as you did earlier.

NATHAN. A damsel in...? I didn't ignore you. I thought I was alone. *(Looks around.)* Where did you come from anyway?

PRINCESS. My castle! Or I should say, what used to be my castle. The dragon destroyed it and is now after me. Can you please help me?

NATHAN *(smiles)*. Wait a second. I think I know what's going on here! Did Bethany put you up to this? *(He looks around.)*

PRINCESS. I'm sorry. But I really have no idea what you're talking about. There is no one named Bethany in my village. Please understand, time is of the essence. If we don't act soon, we are both going to be dragon food!

NATHAN. Dragon food. *(He laughs.)* You're good! Hey, weren't you in *Guys and Dolls* last fall? Bethany played Adelaide. I really liked that song, oh, what's it called? Oh yeah, "Take Back Your Mink." The girls took off their—

PRINCESS. You are certainly trying my patience.

NATHAN You totally had me fooled! You could be a princess, you know it? Hmmm. Now I've got to think of some way to trick Bethany.

PRINCESS. I was right. You are the village idiot.

NATHAN *(laughs)*. The village idiot! That's a good one! *(Continues laughing.)*

PRINCESS *(looks offstage and is terrified. She moves behind NATHAN and covers herself with her cape)*. I beg of you, don't tell him where I am!

NATHAN. Who?

PRINCESS. The dragon!

NATHAN. Oh yeah, right. The dragon! *(He laughs.)*

PRINCESS. Don't move!

NATHAN *(amused)*. Okay, I won't!

(DRAGON flies onstage. He roars loudly. Shocked, NA-THAN freezes.)

DRAGON *(sees NATHAN and flies over to him)*. Who...
are...you? *(NATHAN continues holding very still hoping the DRAGON will just disappear.)* I said, who are
you? *(NATHAN. closes his eyes. Still doesn't move.)*
BOO!

NATHAN. Aughhh!

*(DRAGON laughs. He takes a deep breath, and then
tries to blow fire at NATHAN. NATHAN tries to protect
himself with his hands.)*

DRAGON. Nuts. My fire is out. That was a big castle.
Took a lot out of me. Tell me, whatever your name is,
have you perchance seen Princess Elizabeth in these
woods?

NATHAN. Me? No. No princess.

DRAGON. Are you certain?

NATHAN. Yeah...I'm sure.

DRAGON. Because if I come back here and discover that
you have lied to me, it will be very bad for you.

NATHAN. Yes, I mean, no! She's not here.

DRAGON. Well, if you do see her, please tell her the
dragon is looking for her. And when I find her—

NATHAN. I'll tell her. If I see her, that is. Which is doubt-
ful. *(DRAGON leans in closer to NATHAN and growls.)*
But possible! I mean, anything's possible, right?
(Laughs nervously.)

DRAGON. Hmmm. *(He studies NATHAN carefully.)* Very
well. Until we meet again! *(He flies off.)*

NATHAN *(finally relaxes. To PRINCESS)*. Man, I thought
you were kidding me! He really is a dragon, isn't he?

PRINCESS *(steps out from behind him)*. Of course! Why would I have told you otherwise? And please do not refer to me as a "man." I am, as you can see, a lady. A princess, to be precise.

NATHAN *(to himself)*. What is happening? I wonder if I blew out some of my brain cells with my volume cranked up. Mom always said that would happen.

PRINCESS. You certainly speak strangely.

NATHAN. Where did you come from anyway?

PRINCESS. Me? Why my castle, of course! My you are a silly village idiot.

NATHAN. I'm not sure what's going on here, but I have to tell you, I'm getting really freaked out. Whoever you are, you seem to be bad news. And not very grateful. I'm pretty sure I just saved you from a dragon. Or a delusional guy who thinks he's a dragon. Either way, I don't appreciate being called an idiot. *(He begins to walk away.)*

PRINCESS *(rushes after him)*. Wait! I'm sorry! I just assumed watching you earlier—

NATHAN. Watching me?

PRINCESS. When you were doing that ridiculous thing with your— *(She acts out his air guitar.)*

NATHAN. My air guitar?

PRINCESS. Excuse me?

NATHAN. My...oh, never mind. I need to get going. Bethany gets really ticked off when I'm late.

PRINCESS. You're just going to leave me here? With no protection whatsoever?

NATHAN. I'm sure you can find a village idiot to help you. *(He begins to walk away.)*

PRINCESS *(runs to him)*. Wait! Please forgive me! I'm not sure what is happening either, but I'm begging for your help. My castle is in ruins, I don't know if there are any survivors, and you are the only person I have seen!

NATHAN. Do you swear you're telling the truth?

PRINCESS. Yes! Why would you doubt me?

NATHAN. I can think of a few reasons.

PRINCESS. Come with me to my castle. I'll prove it to you. We'll need to be very careful though. I'm sure the dragon will be going back there soon.

NATHAN. Well…

PRINCESS. Please. *(She moves in closer to him and smiles sweetly.)*

NATHAN *(realizes how lovely she is)*. I, uh, I need to call my girlfriend first. *(He takes out his cell phone.)*

PRINCESS. Oh, thank you, kind sir! I'll help you! *(Turns away from him and calls out.)* Princess Bethany! Oh, Princess Bethany! Your prince is going with me to see my ruined castle and save me from a dragon!

NATHAN *(startled, stares at PRINCESS. He holds up his phone)*. I meant on my phone.

PRINCESS. Your what?

NATHAN. My—

PRINCESS. What a curious little thing!

NATHAN *(to himself)*. Wow. I think she's serious. *(To PRINCESS.)* This village you come from. Is it isolated from the rest of the world?

PRINCESS. Oh my, yes. We've had many enemies for hundreds of years. We live on fertile land, but even more importantly, we own more gold and jewels than any other kingdom.

NATHAN. Excuse me a second. *(He calls BETHANY on phone. PRINCESS watches with great interest.)* Hey, babe. *(He holds phone away from his ear. BETHANY is yelling.)* Uh, Bethany? *(Yelling.)* Bethy? *(Yelling.)* Are you done? Good. Here's the thing. I'm running late and… *(Yelling.)*

(PRINCESS tries to help NATHAN by taking his phone. NATHAN tries to get it back, but she moves about so that he is unable to.)

PRINCESS. Excuse me? Princess Bethany, is it? What a lovely name. I am Princess Elizabeth. Prince Nathan has agreed to help me escape from the dragon and help me back to my village. So he will be unable to meet with you today. *(She holds phone away. To NATHAN.)* Goodness! I'm not sure what she is saying, but it certainly doesn't sound very nice! *(She gives him back his phone.)*

NATHAN *(nervously puts phone to his ear)*. Bethany? Honey? Great. She hung up.

PRINCESS. Hung up what?

NATHAN. Never mind. I'm not looking forward to seeing her anytime soon.

PRINCESS. Your princess?

NATHAN. Believe me, she's no princess.

PRINCESS. Have your parents arranged your marriage?

NATHAN. Marriage?

PRINCESS. Of course.

NATHAN. God, no! Our parents don't arrange our marriages. We choose who we marry. Which I hope will never happen in my case.

PRINCESS. You are a very confusing man.

NATHAN. Confusing, maybe. Confused, yes. *(Smiles at her and takes her hand.)* Now let's go and find your castle.

PRINCESS. Oh, thank you, Prince Nathan!

NATHAN. Prince Nathan. Hmmm. I kind of like that!

(They run offstage.

DRAGON flies onstage and looks around. He roars.)

DRAGON. Princess? Oh, Princess? I had a delicious main course, but now I need my dessert! *(He looks around.)* Come out, come out, wherever you are! Drat! She's not here. Well, she can't have gone far. And I have all the patience in the world! Off to check the castle! Or what's left of it! *(He laughs and flies offstage.)*

(BETHANY storms onstage. She's furious. She looks around.)

BETHANY. Nathan! Where are you? Oh, and please be sure to introduce me to Princess Elizabeth! I can't wait to gouge her royal eyes out! NATHAN!!! *(She runs off.)*

(PRINCESS enters holding NATHAN's hand. She points.)

PRINCESS. There it is. My castle. Ruined.

NATHAN *(sees it)*. Holy crap.

PRINCESS. Excuse me?

NATHAN. You weren't lying, were you?

PRINCESS. Why would I lie? My beautiful home. *(She begins to cry.)*

NATHAN *(puts his arms around her).* Something very strange is happening here.

DRAGON *(flies on).* Aha! I thought you said you hadn't seen the princess!

NATHAN *(puts PRINCESS behind him and summons all his courage).* Don't you think you've done enough damage for one day?

DRAGON. My, you seem to have acquired a little more courage than the last time I saw you! Now, step away from the princess and I might let you live for five more minutes.

NATHAN. I think not, you overgrown reptile!

PRINCESS. Watch out, Prince Nathan!

NATHAN. Get behind that boulder, Princess!

PRINCESS *(she does).* Be careful, dear Prince!

(BETHANY storms onstage. She has overheard PRIN-CESS.)

BETHANY. By all means, be careful, Prince.

NATHAN. Bethany! What are you doing here?

BETHANY. Looking for my two-timing boyfriend, that's what!

NATHAN. Get back! This dragon is dangerous!

BETHANY. What dragon?

DRAGON *(steps in front of her).* You're two-timing boy-friend is referring to me.

BETHANY. Whatever. Get out of my way, knucklehead.

NATHAN *(warning)*. Bethany—

(DRAGON and BETHANY look at each other. They are instantly attracted to each another.)

DRAGON. I've always liked a princess with spunk. How do you feel about flying?

BETHANY. Beats the bus.

DRAGON *(laughs)*. Beats the bus. Good one! *(Realizes.)* What's a bus?

NATHAN. Uh, Bethany?

BETHANY. You look very strong. Do you work out?

DRAGON. I am very strong.

BETHANY. I can see that. I'll bet you don't leave your girlfriend waiting while you run around with some princess.

DRAGON. Of course not. Why, I am as true as my word. Would you like to go for a ride?

BETHANY. You know…I would. *(She looks at NATHAN.)* There is nothing left for me here.

DRAGON. Hop on, sweet lady.

BETHANY. Don't mind if I do! *(She hops on his back. They fly offstage.)*

(PRINCESS comes out of hiding.)

PRINCESS. Goodness. That must have been heartbreaking for you.

NATHAN. Surprisingly, it wasn't. Just a little gross I guess.

PRINCESS. Gross. What a funny word. Well, I don't think the dragon will be bothering us anymore!

NATHAN. Apparently Bethany won't be either!

PRINCESS *(looks offstage and smiles, waves)*. Look! It's my parents! They're all right!

NATHAN. Oh my gosh. It really is!

PRINCESS. Come and meet them!

NATHAN. Hop on, sweet lady!

PRINCESS. Don't mind if I do! *(She hops on his back. They exit.)*

BLACKOUT

THE DRAMAS

Barbie Girl

No pe

A girl surrounds herself with Barbie dolls in her attempt to hide a painful secret.

CHARACTERS:

JILL. . . . . Innocent and childlike. Very sincere.
She has a terrible secret that she is dealing with
in the only way she knows how.

BRIDGET. . . . . . . Good sense of humor. A bit sarcastic.
She is visiting Jill's house for the first time.
She quickly realizes something is very wrong with Jill,
but decides to stay anyway.

* * * *

AT RISE: *JILL is surrounded by eighteen Barbie dolls. She hums a song while brushing a doll's hair.*

JILL *(to her dolls).* We're having company today. I made a friend at school and she should be here soon. Now, I expect you to all be on your best behavior. Clarissa and McKenzie, you look beautiful today! Barbie, are you warm enough? *(She listens to Barbie.)* Oh, good. *(Listens.)* Thank you, Barbie. I'm glad you like it. I wanted to look nice for my new friend, Bridget. *(Notices.)* Midge! Why are you over there? I specifically told you to stay beside Barbie in case— *(She looks around.)* Well, you know why. You can never be too careful, and I can't watch her every second. *(She moves Midge.)* There. Keep an eye out. *(She looks around.)* Oh no! I forgot the car! Be right back! *(She runs offstage.)*

(BRIDGET enters. She walks up to "door" and calls out.)

BRIDGET. Hello!

JILL *(from offstage)*. Bridget?

BRIDGET. Yeah. Jill? The door's open so I just...

JILL. Come on in! I'll be right there!

BRIDGET. Okay! *(She enters house and looks around.)* Nice house!

(JILL enters holding a Barbie car.)

JILL. Thanks!

BRIDGET *(looks at toy car)*. Does your car get good gas mileage?

JILL. What? No, this isn't my...I mean, it's Barbie's car.

BRIDGET. Uh-huh... So, does she get good gas mileage?

JILL *(confused)*. I don't—

BRIDGET. I'm joking, Jill!

JILL. Oh. Oh! Of course! *(She laughs.)*

BRIDGET. Are you babysitting your little sister or some-thing?

JILL. I don't have a little sister. *(Beat.)* Why?

BRIDGET *(looks around at the dolls)*. Uh, well, let's see. There are about a hundred Barbie dolls lying around. I just thought you must be...

JILL. Eighteen.

BRIDGET. Excuse me?

JILL. You said a hundred. There are only eighteen. Here, I mean. I have a lot more. Do you want to see them?

BRIDGET. Wait. These are yours?

JILL. Yes. Aren't they beautiful?

BRIDGET. Yeah, but, uh…

JILL. I've collected them for years.

BRIDGET *(relieved)*. Oh, you collect them. Wow. For a second there I thought you…

JILL *(picks up doll)*. My favorite is Birthday Barbie. Guess when I got her?

BRIDGET. Your birthday?

JILL. Right!

BRIDGET. Lucky guess…

JILL. Look at her dress.

BRIDGET. Yeah, it's uh, it's really poofy.

JILL. Poofy?

BRIDGET. Yeah, you know. Big.

JILL. But it's beautiful, isn't it?

BRIDGET. I guess. If you like poofy dresses.

JILL. I do! I hope that I can get a dress like this someday. She's a collectible.

BRIDGET. A what?

JILL. A collectible. She's worth a lot. I usually keep her in her box. But I decided today was a special day, so… here she is! Do you want to hold her?

BRIDGET. Uh…

JILL. You're the first person I've ever let hold her.

BRIDGET. Oh. Well…okay.

JILL. Be very careful. *(Demonstrating.)* You hold her under her dress.

BRIDGET. But I barely know her.

JILL. What?

BRIDGET. I said I barely...never mind.

JILL. Oh, I get it! *(Laughs. Hands her the doll.)*

BRIDGET. That's makes one of us. *(Carefully holds doll as JILL demonstrated.)* Like this?

JILL. Yes. Now you can really see how beautiful she is.

BRIDGET. Are you...?

JILL. Am I what?

BRIDGET. I'm just trying to figure this out, that's all.

JILL. Figure what out?

BRIDGET. This whole doll obsession thing.

JILL. Don't you have Barbies?

BRIDGET. Not anymore. I mean, I might have a few left over from when I was little, but uh...I don't play with them anymore.

JILL. That's too bad.

BRIDGET. Why? I never really played with them when I was little either. I'm more of a bike-riding, skateboarding, tree-climbing kind of girl.

JILL. They make Barbies that do all of that!

BRIDGET. Really.

JILL. Yes, do you want to see some?

BRIDGET. No thanks. *(Hands doll back to JILL.)* Here, this is making me nervous. I might drop her or something.

JILL *(carefully takes Barbie and puts her into the Barbie car)*. Now she can get away.

BRIDGET. Get away?

JILL. Yes. I mean, if she has to. You never know. *(She carefully adjusts Barbie's dress in the car.)*

BRIDGET. No, I guess you never do. *(Watches JILL. Uncomfortable pause.)* You know, I've got a lot of homework. I should probably go.

JILL *(hurt)*. But you just got here! We've really been looking forward to getting to know you! I mean I have.

BRIDGET *(considers for a moment)*. Well, I...

JILL. Please? It'll be so much fun!

BRIDGET. Jill, I don't want to hurt your feelings or anything, but I really don't want to play with dolls.

JILL. Well, of course you don't! We're too old for that! But can't I just tell you a little bit about them?

BRIDGET. All one hundred of them?

JILL. But there are only... Oh! You're joking again, aren't you?

BRIDGET. Yep.

JILL. You're so funny, Bridget!

BRIDGET. A regular stand-up comedian. That's me. *(Looks at watch and decides.)* I have about twenty minutes, but then I really have to go, all right?

JILL. All right. I was hoping you could stay longer, but maybe another time.

BRIDGET. Maybe. *(Pause.)* So tell me about your doll fixation.

JILL. The reason I love Barbies is because they are perfect in every way.

BRIDGET. I think there are a few million women who would beg to differ on that point. They don't exactly set a realistic standard for young girls. I read somewhere that if Barbies were life-sized, their measurements would be something like 38-18-34. If she were real she'd be anorexic. Not to mention the fact that she'd fall over from boob overload.

JILL. No offense, Bridget, but you don't know what you're talking about. Barbie is the perfect woman.

BRIDGET. Please tell me you're not serious. *(JILL looks at BRIDGET. She's serious.)* Wow. Okay. Enlighten me. Because frankly I'm getting a little freaked out.

JILL. I can only tell you how I feel. I realize that I don't speak for everyone.

BRIDGET. As long as we agree on that.

JILL. Is that another joke?

BRIDGET. Of course.

JILL *(laughs)*. I'm so glad you came over today. I don't have any friends, and I'm just so…happy you're here. It means a lot to me, Bridget.

BRIDGET. Oh, well. Sure. I'm uh, you bet. *(Beat.)* You don't have any friends?

JILL. Nope. Not one. I know people think I'm weird, but I can't help it. Mother said that's just the way God made me.

BRIDGET. Jill. I don't think God made people so they wouldn't have any friends. I mean, it can be hard making friends. You have to put yourself out there, and sometimes you realize that you have nothing in common with that person. So you just keep trying.

JILL *(happy)*. I did. And here you are!

BRIDGET. Right. *(Beat.)* You were telling me about how perfect Barbie is.

JILL. Of course she is! She doesn't need to eat, she will always be beautiful, and most importantly, she doesn't feel pain.

BRIDGET. Well, you got me there.

JILL. She has a beautiful home, she can work if she wants to, but she doesn't have to. She's always smiling, and she has all of these friends. *(Smiles at the dolls.)*

BRIDGET. What about Ken?

JILL *(winces)*. What about him?

BRIDGET. I just noticed you don't have any boy dolls. I wanted to see him naked.

JILL. That's disgusting, Bridget! Seriously!

BRIDGET *(laughs)*. Come on, Jill. I'm just kidding! Besides, the last time I saw a naked Ken doll, there wasn't much there to write home about. I'm just curious if he's grown with the times.

JILL *(upset)*. I wouldn't know.

BRIDGET. Jill, come on. I was totally joking around. It's what I do. *(Looks around.)* So, do you have siblings?

JILL. Not at home.

BRIDGET. Parents?

JILL. At work.

BRIDGET. Oh. So older sibs at school?

JILL *(pause)*. Just one. He's away.

BRIDGET. Okay. *(Pause.)* Maybe I should go.

JILL. No, please.

BRIDGET. But you seem mad at me.

JILL. No. I'm not. Really.

BRIDGET. Well, I said something that upset you. *(JILL begins to cry.)* Jill, please tell me. What is it?

JILL. I can't. I just can't. *(Looks at her dolls.)* I'll tell you about Barbie though, all right?

BRIDGET. All right.

(JILL gets her Barbie and Midge dolls. She hands Midge to BRIDGET and holds Barbie. BRIDGET real-

izes something is seriously wrong, She carefully holds Midge and faces JILL.)

JILL *(speaks as Barbie)*. Hi, Midge.

BRIDGET *(as Midge)*. Hi...Barbie.

JILL. You look very nice today.

BRIDGET. Thank you. So do you.

JILL. It's my birthday.

BRIDGET. Happy birthday.

JILL. Thanks.

BRIDGET. You look kind of sad considering it's your birthday.

JILL. I do?

BRIDGET. A little bit. Is something wrong?

JILL. No. Everything is perfect. Do you want to go for a ride?

BRIDGET. Okay.

(They put dolls in car and push it back and forth as they continue talking.)

JILL. It sure is a lovely day.

BRIDGET. It sure is. *(She pushes car faster.)* Wheee!

JILL *(nervous)*. We can't go too fast. We might get pulled over.

BRIDGET. By who? *(An uncomfortable pause as BRIDGET waits for JILL to answer. She doesn't.)* I'll protect you, Barbie.

JILL. You didn't the last time. Or the time before that.

(BRIDGET realizes. She takes Midge out of car and hands Barbie to JILL. They continue talking through the dolls.)

BRIDGET. I'm sorry, Barbie. I let you down. *(Looks around.)* Where is he?

JILL. At a place where they teach boys they can't do that to their sisters.

BRIDGET *(stunned. She fights to stay calm for JILL)*. Well, that's good, isn't it? I mean…at least he's not around.

JILL. He gets out in a month. Then what? *(Beat.)* I want to stay a doll forever. It's perfect being a doll.

BRIDGET. Yeah. I can understand that now. But it can be pretty good being you, too. Especially if you have a friend you can talk to.

JILL. Do you mean it, Midge? Will you be my friend even if everyone thinks I'm weird?

BRIDGET *(puts doll down. As herself)*. Yes, Jill. I'll be your friend. Especially if people think you're weird. *(She smiles.)* I've got a reputation to uphold you know.

(JILL breaks down. BRIDGET comforts her while she cries.)

BLACKOUT

Danny

Three sisters visit their brother's gravesite on the one-year anniversary of his death.

CHARACTERS:

JULIE . . Oldest sister. Tries to stay strong for her younger siblings, especially Mel.

LAYLA . . . . Middle sister. Uses humor to cope with loss.

MEL . . . . Youngest sister. Danny's twin. She is still devastated by her brother's death.

* * * *

AT RISE: *GIRLS enter. LAYLA is carrying a picnic basket and JULIE is carrying a blanket. MEL is trying not to cry. They glance at a few of the "gravestones."*

JULIE. He's over there.
LAYLA. I see him.

(They arrive at their brother's gravesite. They stand and look at it for a moment. MEL wipes her eyes. JULIE and LAYLA put their arms around her.)

JULIE. You okay, Mel?

MEL. Yeah. *(Shakes her head.)* No. *(She begins to cry.)*
(JULIE and LAYLA comfort MEL.)

LAYLA. It's all right.
JULIE. Here. *(She places blanket on ground.)* Do you want
to sit?
MEL. In a minute. I'm sorry. I told myself I wasn't going
to do this.
JULIE. Cry? We're all going to do that. Don't apologize.

(GIRLS look at the gravestone.)

MEL. Hi, Danny. I sure miss you.
LAYLA. Hey, Danny.
JULIE. Your sisters are all here.
LAYLA. I seriously can't believe it's been a year.
JULIE. Me either.

*(MEL moves closer to gravestone and runs her fingers
along the "inscription.")*

MEL. I miss you every second. How many seconds are in
a year? I miss you so much, Danny. You were the best
brother we could have ever asked for. *(She sits on blanket. SISTERS follow. MEL smiles.)* Remember how
Danny and I would always end up wearing the same
color of clothes in the morning without planning it?
LAYLA. That was crazy. You actually had to plan what to
wear the night before so you *didn't* match.
JULIE. I thought it was cute.
MEL. I did too. But I know Danny's friends gave him a
hard time about it.

LAYLA. Anyone hungry?

(JULIE and MEL look at her strangely.)

JULIE. You've always had weird timing, Layla.

LAYLA. So I've heard. Pudding cup, Mel? It's butter-scotch. Danny's…and your favorite.

MEL. Maybe later. Do you remember when Danny was really into his magician phase?

JULIE. Oh, yeah.

LAYLA. I was mad at him 'cause he kept taking our stuff to try and make it disappear. The only place it disappeared from was our rooms.

MEL. But he got really good.

JULIE. He did.

MEL *(as if announcing him onstage)*. "The Great Danbeani!"

LAYLA. Not the best stage name. It always sounded like he was swearing.

JULIE. He was young. He got his n's and m's mixed up a lot.

MEL. My favorite was when we were five and the whole family was together. I think it was Thanksgiving. We sat down for dinner and Danny ran in wearing his magic hat and cape. Dad said, "Danny, please take off your costume for dinner." Then Danny announced, "The Great Dam-beani must be ready to perform at all times!" *(GIRLS laugh.)* And then he started pulling that scarf out of his sleeve…

LAYLA. It was like a mile long!

JULIE. Seriously, I never figured out how he stuffed that whole thing up his little sleeve!

MEL. I know! Grandma said: "Did Danny just swear?" We were laughing and encouraging him. But Dad was being, well, Dad and he said, "Danny, will you please do your trick after dinner? It's getting cold." But Danny just kept pulling out his scarf and without missing a beat he said, "The great Dam-beani must continue!" Dad was getting mad, but everyone else thought it was so cute that he finally gave in. By now the scarf was changing colors as it came out. Aunt Marion kept naming all the colors: "Red! Oh look, blue! Now it's yellow!" I think it was after purple that Danny looked at me and said, "And now for some assistance from my lovely assistance!" I ran over and helped him pull the rest of the scarf out. When we were done, Danny took my hand and we bowed. You all clapped and smiled and yelled "Bravo!" I'll never forget the look on Danny's face. Pure and utter joy. I felt...complete. Like we were one person. And I knew in that second, even at the age of five, that life would never, ever get better than that moment. And you know what? I was right.

(Silent moment as they all reflect.)

JULIE. I'll never forget it either, Mel. I wish I had a video of that moment, but you know it wouldn't be the same. You were both so cute, and I could tell you were the proudest sister in the world.

LAYLA. I was jealous. I mean, you know, a little bit. I used to wish that Danny was my twin. Especially the way you'd finish each other's sentences. I always thought that was so cool.

MEL. Yeah, I think a lot of twins do that. I'm just so grateful to have my sisters. I don't know what I'd do without you.

LAYLA. When are Mom and Dad coming?

JULIE. About half an hour. I wanted us to have some sister time first.

LAYLA. Good thinking.

MEL. Very good thinking. It's torture watching their faces when they're here.

LAYLA. No kidding. Their only son.

(Silent moment.)

JULIE. I feel like Danny's right here with us. I really do.

MEL. I want to feel that, Julie.

LAYLA. Me too.

JULIE. I know. It comes and goes. But right now, I swear he's with us.

(They take a moment.)

LAYLA. Sometimes I smell him. He always smelled so good.

JULIE. Really?

MEL. Where?

LAYLA. Home, school—different places. I'll be going through my day, and suddenly I just smell him. I've actually turned around and expected to see him when it happens.

MEL. He said he'd always be with us.

JULIE. And he will. I guess if there's an up side to getting cancer, it's the fact that you can tell your family things you wouldn't be able to otherwise.

LAYLA. God I hate that word. You know how some words just make you feel like what they are? Cancer is definitely one of them. *(She begins to cry.)*

JULIE. It sure is.

LAYLA. Can I have a Kleenex, Mel?

MEL. Of course. *(She gives her one.)*

LAYLA. I'm not even crying about Danny. Well, of course I am, but last night my wonderful boyfriend of three years broke up with me because, as he put it: "You'll be better off."

MEL. What?

JULIE. Oh no. I'm so sorry, Layla.

LAYLA. Thanks. I wasn't going to talk about this. Not on Danny's anniversary.

JULIE. Of course you need to talk about it.

MEL. Why'd he break up with you?

LAYLA. My suspicion is named Clara.

JULIE. Clara, as in the ditzy-cheerleader Clara?

LAYLA. Yep. She's ditzy, but she's got great pom poms.

MEL *(angry)*. What a jerkaramous!

(JULIE and LAYLA are startled by MEL's sudden outburst. They laugh.)

LAYLA. Jerkaramous?

MEL. Well, yeah! You've always been there for him. Like when his parents split up and his dog ran away and he couldn't pass his stupid biology class. I mean come on!

You are beautiful and smart, talented and funny, and…this just sucks!

LAYLA. Aw, Mel. You're so sweet. *(She hugs her.)* I'd forgotten about that biology class. He'd have never passed it without me. *(Laughs.)* I'd like to see pom pom girl help him with his homework.

JULIE. So, just for the record, is a jerkaramous a type of dinosaur?

MEL. It's whatever you want it to be. Danny and I always made up names for people. Dorkus mahorkus was one of my all-time favorites.

LAYLA. Dorkus mahorkus?

MEL. A serious dork.

JULIE. Obviously.

MEL. Danny made that one up for you, Layla.

LAYLA. What?

MEL. I think it was when you decided to charge us all for your sage advice.

JULIE. Oh yeah, you were definitely a dorkus mahorkus back then. You put a sign on your door with your rates. Fifty cents for fashion advice.

MEL. Two dollars for boyfriend advice.

LAYLA. I gave a money-back guarantee!

JULIE. One dollar for how to get Dad to say "yes."

LAYLA. That was a bargain.

JULIE. True.

LAYLA *(to the gravestone)*. Danny, I wish you'd stick up for me. I know you would.

JULIE. I know he would, too.

MEL. Definitely.

LAYLA. Time for Danny's favorites.

JULIE. Danny's favorite song.

MEL & LAYLA. "Puff the Magic Dragon"!

JULIE. Favorite food.

MEL. SpaghettiOs. Favorite color.

JULIE & LAYLA. Blue.

LAYLA. Favorite book.

MEL. "Sister for Sale" by Shel Silverstein.

LAYLA. Wait, what?

MEL. It's a short story from *Where the Sidewalk Ends*. It's about a kid who wants to sell his sister.

JULIE. Can't blame him for that one. One of him, three of us.

LAYLA. True. I brought something. But I'm going to need a little help.

MEL. What is it?

(LAYLA opens picnic basket and takes out a long magician's ribbon. MEL and JULIE gasp.)

LAYLA. In honor of our dear brother, Danny, I would like to have his twin sister, Mel, do the honors of his famous scarf trick.

MEL *(picks up the scarf)*. Where did you find it?

LAYLA. In a box in the garage.

JULIE. Kleenex, please.

MEL. In my purse. *(She begins to stuff the scarf up her sleeve.)* I could have sworn this was so much longer!

LAYLA. I know. But it's the perfect length.

JULIE. Yes, it is.

MEL. In honor of the Great Danbeani, I will now perform his famous scarf trick! *(She slowly takes out the scarf.)*

(LAYLA and JULIE "oooh" and "ahhh." They might say the colors as they appear.)

MEL. And now I need some assistance from my lovely assistance. Or should I say, a-sisters.

(LAYLA and JULIE help to take out the rest of the scarf. They wrap the scarf around themselves and smile gently.)

BLACKOUT

I'll Be Seeing You (originally *Felo-De-Se*) was first produced by FAIR School Downtown. It premiered January 12, 2012, at the New Century Theatre City Center in Minneapolis, Minn., with the following:

CAST (Male)

STEVE . . . . Xavier Heim
JOSH . . . . Anthony Morantz

CAST (Female)

STEVIE. . . . . Avery Ellis
JOSIE. . . . . Lydia Sharpe

PRODUCTION STAFF & CREW

Artistic Director . . . . Sandy Boren-Barrett
Director . . . . Adam Hegg
Set/Props Designer. . . . . Jim Hibbeler
Lighting/Technical Director. . . . . Gretchen Katt
Costume Designer. . . . . Shannon O'Black
Stage Manager. . . . . Jenny Moeller
Assistant Stage Manager/Production Manager. . . . Melanie Salmon-Peterson

I'll Be Seeing You

Two friends are reunited briefly a week after one of them committed suicide.

CHARACTERS:

NOTE: This play may be performed with 2 men or 2 women. Dialogue that has been changed for women is written in brackets after the men's line.

STEVE / RACHEL.... A popular and fun-loving boy/girl who killed himself/herself.

JOSH / AVERY ...... His/Her best friend who is trying to understand how Steve/Avery could have done this.

* * * *

AT RISE: *STEVE (RACHEL) is onstage and looks around as if he's not sure where he is.*

JOSH (AVERY) walks onstage and sees STEVE.

JOSH. *(shocked)*. Steve? [Rachel?]
STEVE *(glad to see JOSH)*. Josh! [Avery!]
JOSH. What...what are you doing here?
STEVE. Not sure. I just kind of...you know.
JOSH. No, I really don't.

STEVE. Yeah. *(Awkward silence. Neither is sure what to say.)* How… How've you been?

JOSH *(still in shock)*. Wait, what?

STEVE. I said, how've you been?

JOSH. Are you serious?

STEVE *(smiles)*. Always.

JOSH *(sarcastically)*. That's really funny, man. [That's really funny.]

STEVE. You know me. Life of the party.

JOSH. Yeah. I…uh…I'm in shock at the moment.

STEVE. Understandable. I kind of feel the same way.

JOSH. You do?

STEVE. Yeah.

JOSH. But how did you…

STEVE. Get here?

JOSH. Yeah.

STEVE. No idea. Things have been really strange lately.

JOSH. Yeah?

STEVE. Yeah.

(Silence as they consider what to say.)

JOSH. Why, Steve? [Why, Rachel?]

STEVE. Why what?

JOSH. Seriously? Why what? That's your response?

STEVE. It's as good as anything I can think of.

JOSH. I think you can do a lot better than that. You owe me that much.

STEVE. Sorry I didn't prepare a speech or anything. I didn't think I'd be in this position.

JOSH. Of course you didn't. You never did think things through. You always did whatever you felt like at the time.

STEVE. And your way is so much better? It takes you forever just to make a decision.

JOSH *(angry)*. You were my best friend! Do you know how many years we've known each other? Did you even consider for one second how this would make me feel? Not just me, but everyone! Shit! *(or "Crap!")* I'm so pissed at you! *(He tries to shove STEVE but is unable to actually touch him. It's as if there is an invisible wall between them. He tries again, but the same thing happens. JOSH is surprised by this. He looks at STEVE helplessly.)*

STEVE. I understand.

JOSH. Do you? Are you sure? Because I'm having a really hard time believing that.

STEVE. Look, I don't know what you want me to say.

JOSH. I want to know why.

STEVE. Why? Why. Everyone says that, don't they? Whenever we don't understand something, we say "why" like someone has the answers. Like someone or something actually gives a shit *(crap)*…

JOSH. Is that the reason? Because you don't think anyone cares about you? That you think there's no God?

STEVE. The truth is, sometimes there aren't any answers.

JOSH *(calmer)*. All right. So I take it that you don't have a reason. That it was just something you felt you had to do. Like when you ran away from home. Or the night you climbed that water tower and couldn't get back down. Or when—

STEVE *(interrupts)*. You made your point. I'm impulsive. I already know that.

JOSH. But there's a big difference between being impulsive and being stupid. Did you wake up last week and say to yourself: "Steve, [Rachel] this is the day. I've had it. No more." *(Beat.)* Was it an accident? Because I'd feel a lot better knowing that it was.

STEVE. No.

JOSH. Well, what then?! Come on! You've got to help me out here.

STEVE. Look Josh, [Avery] I'm sorry. I really am. I didn't mean to hurt you.

JOSH. Hurt me? I wish it was just me. It's your family, your friends, your school—there's no way to tell how many people have been damaged by this. For the rest of their lives, Steve. [Rachel.] *(Beat.)* Your mom can't talk. Did you know that?

STEVE *(pause)*. Look, I said I'm sorry. It's not like there's anything I can do about it now.

JOSH. It would help if you would just tell me why.

STEVE. Would it? Would it really? Because I don't think that's true. It doesn't matter why. It's done. No one can possibly understand it unless they've been where I was. So even if I could put it into words for you, it wouldn't be enough.

JOSH. Anything would be better than nothing! Was it your grades? Your parents? Your job? Because we lost the last basketball game? What? You're the most popular guy [girl] in school. Everyone loves you. Everyone. Even Mrs. Farrell! And she hates kids! You're always the first person to a party and the last one to leave. It's not even a party unless you're there. You're like the effing [frickin'] chosen one. What the hell happened? Was it the alcohol? Because you sure had enough of it that night. At least that's what I heard.

STEVE. You really want to know why?

JOSH. Uh, yeah. Have you been listening?

STEVE. All right, all right. *(Beat.)* I never felt the way everyone saw me. I was the first one at parties because I couldn't stand being alone. It was like being in a black elevator that was always going down farther and farther into darkness. I couldn't get out of it. Lately everything just went to shit *(crap)*. Grades, girls, [boys] but mostly my own head. When you saw me smiling and talking I was actually trying to prove to others and myself that I was okay. That I wasn't insane. That I could stop that elevator. But I couldn't. I thought about my future. College. An 8-5 job. The economy. Getting married. Having kids. Getting old. I mean, what the hell is it all for? I knew without a doubt that I could never ever do those things.

JOSH. Nobody can if they look at all of that at once. *(Beat.)* Did you really think you were insane?

STEVE. Yeah. This voice inside of me just kept telling me what a loser I was. Nothing was good enough, nothing. And nothing that I did made any difference because it was all shit *(crap)*. And yes. I did drink a lot that night. But either way I couldn't face another day, man. [Avery.] I just couldn't.

JOSH. You could have called me. Or texted me. You had to know I'd be there for you.

STEVE. Don't do this to yourself. It had nothing to do with you. Or my family. Nobody could have changed my mind.

JOSH. Had you thought about doing it before?

STEVE. Yeah. Lots of times. *(Beat.)* I tried a year ago.

JOSH. What'd you do?

STEVE. Pills. My parents found me and took me to the hospital. *(Laughs.)* I couldn't even do that right.

JOSH. I can't believe you didn't tell me. But let me ask you something. Wasn't this last year worth living?

STEVE. Well, yeah. Some of it was. The state championship for sure. *(Smiles.)* And Jessica was definitely worth it. [And Luke was definitely worth it.]

JOSH. That's my point! If you could have just waited or reached out to someone. God, Steve! [God, Rachel!] Things always get better! Always! Why couldn't you have…?

STEVE. Josh. [Avery.] Listen to me. It's done. It's over. I'm sorry. I really am. I didn't mean to hurt so many people. You were a great friend, man. [You were a great friend.] The best. *(He looks off.)* I have to go.

JOSH. Wait. Will I see you again?

STEVE. No. This was a one-time thing. Hey, you should be glad that I picked you. I could have visited anyone. *(Smiles.)* Even Jessica. [Even Luke.]

(A school bell rings.)

JOSH. Was that a school bell?

STEVE. Yeah.

JOSH. Wait. You go to school?!

STEVE. Yeah. Apparently the way it works is what you don't finish here, you have to finish up there.

JOSH *(laughs)*. That is hilarious! You have to go to school! Unbelievable!

STEVE. Yeah. Hilarious.

JOSH. Wait until I tell— Damn. No one's going to believe this, are they?

STEVE. Doubt it. But tell my family I love them, will you? And tell my mom that her first dog was named Nicki. It was a terrier. It fell down a cliff when she was little and she went down and saved it. Mom never told me that, so she'll believe you saw me. And tell her to start talking again, because I miss her voice, all right?

JOSH. Yeah. I'll tell her.

(School bell rings.)

STEVE. Bye, Josh. [Bye, Avery.]

JOSH. Bye, Steve. [Bye, Rachel.]

STEVE *(begins to walk off. Turns around)*. I'll be seeing you.

JOSH. Yeah. *(Beat.)* Good luck with your classes. And don't try copying off of me, all right?

STEVE. All right. Love you, man. [Love you, Avery.]

JOSH. You too. [You too, Rachel.]

(STEVE exits. JOSH stays and watches him exit.)
[RACHEL exits. AVERY stays and watches her exit.]

BLACKOUT

Late

ALISON meets with her longtime girlfriend, RYAN, at a park. She eventually shares the fact that she might be pregnant.

CHARACTERS:

ALISON . . . . A teenage girl who may be pregnant.

RYAN . . . . Her girlfriend who tries to be supportive.

AT RISE: *ALISON is sitting on a park bench under a tree. She watches "a little girl on a swing." She smiles, and then wipes away tears.*

RYAN enters carrying a picnic basket. She looks around for ALISON.

* * * *

RYAN. There you are, Alison! Are you hiding under this tree?
ALISON. No. I just like the shade. How's it going, Ryan?
RYAN. Great! I love this park.
ALISON. Nice, isn't it?
RYAN. Yeah. This was a great idea! *(Smells the air.)* Smell those flowers!
ALISON *(she does)*. Lilac. My favorite.

RYAN *(sits next to ALISON. Holds up picnic basket).* Brought some goodies!

ALISON. How sweet of you.

RYAN *(looks around).* Aww, look at that little girl on the swing. She's adorable!

ALISON. I know. I've been watching her.

RYAN. She reminds me of you when you were little. Remember how you always wore that little whale spout of a pony tail on the top of your head?

ALISON *(laughs).* That's probably why I get headaches now.

RYAN *(opens her picnic basket).* Grapes?

ALISON. No thanks.

(They watch a very good-looking "guy" walk by.)

RYAN. Nice tatts. *(She begins eating grapes.)*

ALISON. That's not all that's nice. *(They watch him walk off.)* I like it when a guy that looks like that is walking a tiny dog, don't you?

RYAN. He was walking a dog? *(She looks offstage.)*

ALISON *(laughs).* You wouldn't be a good witness at a crime scene.

RYAN. So guess who finally called me?

ALISON. Bryce.

RYAN. How'd you know?

ALISON. You texted it to me last night!

RYAN. I did?

ALISON. Ryan!

RYAN. Oh yeah. I remember now. I was so excited that last night is kind of a blur.

ALISON. So?

RYAN. So what?

ALISON. What'd he say?

RYAN. He asked if he left his jacket in my car when I brought him home from school. *(Offers her a banana.)* Banana?

ALISON. No thanks. *(Beat.)* There has to be more.

RYAN *(looking in basket)*. There is. I've got carrot sticks, apples, and your favorite! Oreos!

ALISON. I meant more to the phone call!

(RYAN smiles mischievously. She takes out a water and Coke and offers them to ALISON.)

ALISON *(cont'd., takes water)*. Thanks. I'm going to hurt you if you don't tell me what he said.

RYAN. Someone isn't very grateful for the feast I packed…

ALISON. I said thanks! Now tell me! (*She has opened her water and holds it over RYAN's head.*)

RYAN. Okay, okay! I told him yes, he did leave his coat in my car.

ALISON. And…?

RYAN. And…he asked me out!

(They scream.)

ALISON. I'm so happy for you! Details!

RYAN. Well, nothing's planned yet, and I'll have to drive because he's in trouble and can't use his dad's car for two weeks, but hopefully we'll go to a movie or something soon.

ALISON. Oh.

RYAN. Oh?

ALISON. Yeah. Oh.

RYAN. What does "oh" mean.

ALISON. It just means...oh. I was hoping for a little more, that's all. You're my best friend, and I don't want you to get hurt.

RYAN. Alison! Don't be such a downer! It's a great first step! I wanted you to be happy for me!

ALISON. I am. I really am. I just...never mind.

RYAN. What? Tell me!

ALISON. I just wish he'd asked you out on a proper date.

RYAN. A "proper date"? You sound like the queen of England.

ALSION. Ryan. You know you have a tendency for settling for less than you deserve. Don't be shy about asking for what you want. That's all. You're my best friend. You deserve to be treated well.

RYAN *(realizes).* You don't think all he wants is his coat back, do you?

ALISON. No! Of course not. He could have just asked you to bring it to school.

RYAN. Yeah. I guess. *(Offers her food.)* Cheese and crackers?

ALISON. No thanks. *(Looks in picnic basket.)* How long are you planning on staying here? A week?

RYAN. This is a park. We're having a picnic. Why aren't you eating?

ALISON. I'm not hungry.

RYAN. Not hungry? You're always hungry! *(Eats a cracker.)* Are you sick? You do look a little pale.

ALISON. I'm fine. I'm just...you know.

RYAN. Actually, I don't know. It's the weirdest thing. Unless people tell me what they're thinking or feeling, I usually can't tell what they're thinking or feeling.

ALISON *(watching little girl on swing)*. I'm...I'm late.

RYAN *(stops eating)*. Late?

ALISON. Yes, Ryan. Late.

RYAN. Oh. *(Realizes.)* Oh god. *(Beat.)* How late?

ALISON. Three weeks.

RYAN. Well, that doesn't mean you're for sure, you know...

ALISON. Pregnant?

RYAN. Yeah.

ALISON. No. Not for sure. It's just...I'm never late. But even more than that, I just have this feeling that I am.

(They watch the little girl on swing in silence.)

RYAN. Have you taken a test?

ALISON. Not yet. I'm scared to. Besides, it's probably too early to tell.

RYAN. Probably. *(Pause.)* What will you do if you are?

ALISON. Not sure. What would you do?

RYAN. Me? I don't know. Besides, it doesn't matter what I'd do. It matters what you want to do. It's your body. Plus you don't even know for sure that you're...

ALISON. Pregnant? You can say the word, Ryan. *(Smiles.)* Just not too loud.

RYAN. Sorry. I feel like I'll jinx you if I say it. My point is, why worry about it if you're not sure?

ALISON. Right. Why worry.

RYAN. I thought you guys were...using, uh...

ALISON. Protection?

RYAN. Yeah.

ALISON. We do. Most of the time.

RYAN. Oh. Does Logan know?

ALISON. He knows I'm late.

RYAN. What'd he say?

ALISON. He said he'll support me no matter what.

RYAN. Well, that's good, right? I mean, a lot of guys wouldn't be there.

ALISON. He was there all right. *(They laugh weakly. ALISON begins to cry.)*

RYAN. Oh, Ali. I'm so sorry. I'm such a selfish friend. I talked on and on about Bryce and his stupid jacket, and how maybe I'm going on a date with him, and all this time you've been worrying about whether or not your life is going to change forever.

ALISON. You're not selfish. You're my best friend. And you're the only person I can talk to about this. Seriously, I don't know what I'd do otherwise.

RYAN *(hands ALISON a tissue)*. Do you think you could talk to your mom?

ALISON. You're kidding, right?

RYAN. I know your parents have pretty strong beliefs, but I just mean if it comes down to needing an adult…

ALISON. Strong beliefs? Ryan. My parents have an impenetrable force field around their beliefs. So the answer to your well-meaning question is no. I can't talk to my mom, dad, grandparents or even our family dog about this. *(Silence. ALISON begins to laugh.)*

RYAN. What?

ALISON. You do remember who taught me about sex, don't you?

RYAN. Oh no. Here it comes.

ALISON. That's right. It was you and your brilliant Barbie and Ken demo. Now that I think about it, you're at least partially responsible for this.

RYAN. You're never going to let me live that down, are you?

ALISON. Of course not! Some things are indelibly etched into our minds for all time. We were in my back yard, remember?

RYAN. I plead the fifth.

ALISON. Ken brought Barbie some dandelions. You told me it was important that a man and woman only have sex with someone they love and preferably are married to. The next thing I know, they're naked and rolling around in the yard. Mom opened the back door and asked what we were doing and you threw Ken into the daisies, remember? *(She and RYAN laugh.)*

RYAN. That's right! Then she came outside with some lemonade. When she saw your naked Barbie, your mom asked why she didn't have any clothes on. You told her you didn't want to get grass stains on her dress.

ALISON. Which would have worked if my trusty Golden Retriever, Chloe, hadn't retrieved Ken and dropped him at her feet.

RYAN. That was unfortunate.

ALISON. But all mom said was to put their clothes back on before they caught pneumonia. *(They laugh. ALISON looks at the little girl on swing.)* Oh, look at her now.

RYAN. She's so cute. Do you realize that we've known each other since we were her age?

ALISON. That's true. We are getting old.

RYAN. Well, you are.

ALISON *(still watching little girl)*. It might not be the worst thing in the world if I am pregnant. I mean, look at her. How hard could it be? Plus there's always adoption I guess.

RYAN. Ali, you'll be fine no matter what happens. You've got me, Logan, your family who, despite what you think, will stand by you. Things could be a lot worse.

ALISON. Yeah. And I might not be pregnant. *(Beat.)* I hope I'm not. I really, really hope I'm not.

RYAN. I hope you're not too. But I'm just saying, either way, you're going to make it.

ALISON. Thanks, Ryan.

RYAN. You bet.

ALISON. Can I have some cheese and crackers now? I finally have an appetite.

RYAN. It's about time!

(She hands ALISON some food. They ad lib as lights fade.)

BLACKOUT

Principal

Two parents have been summoned to bring their kids to PRINCIPAL's office without knowing why.

CHARACTERS:

PRINCIPAL (w). . . . . High school principal.

ADAM QUINN . . . . Father of Cody. Impatient.
                                        Used to being in charge.

CODY QUINN . . . . . Son of Adam. Basically a good kid,
                                        but has made some bad choices.

EMMA RICHARDSON. . . . . Mother of Twilight.
                                        Protective of her daughter.

TWILIGHT RICHARDSON. . . . . . . Daughter of Emma.
            Has been bullying a girl who she thinks has been
                                        hitting on her boyfriend.

2 GUARDS (m/w) . . . . Strong, intimidating.

* * * *

AT RISE: *ADAM and CODY are sitting in an office. There are three other empty chairs and a small table which is PRINCIPAL's desk.*

ADAM. The least you could do is give me some idea why we're here!

CODY. I told you, Dad, I don't know!

ADAM. Of course you know! Your teacher had to give you a reason for sending you to the principal's office!

CODY. Well, she didn't.

ADAM. This is just great. I'm going to feel like an idiot. What's the new principal's name again?

CODY. Just Principal.

ADAM. Cody! What is wrong with you? Her name can't possibly be "Principal"!

(EMMA and TWILIGHT enter.)

EMMA *(to TWILIGHT)*. Is this Principal's office?

TWILIGHT. Yeah.

EMMA *(to ADAM)*. Hi. Are you here for the meeting?

ADAM. Unfortunately.

EMMA. So are we. *(They sit down. There is an uncomfortable silence. To ADAM.)* I'm Emma. And this is my daughter, Twilight.

ADAM. You're kidding.

EMMA. About what?

ADAM. Your daughter's name is Twilight like in the vampire books?

EMMA. Clearly we didn't name her after the books. She was born before they were written.

CODY. Hey, Twilight.

TWILIGHT. Hey, Cody.

ADAM. Sorry. Cute name. So, do you have any idea why we're here?

EMMA. Obviously our kids are in some kind of trouble.

ADAM. Obviously. *(To EMMA.)* Do you know what they did?

EMMA. No, do you?

ADAM. No. My son won't tell me.

EMMA. Twilight won't tell me either.

(PRINCIPAL enters smiling.)

PRINCIPAL. Sorry I'm late. Thank you for coming on such short notice. I'm Principal. *(She puts a file folder on table.)*

ADAM. Principal…?

PRINCIPAL. Correct. You must be Cody's dad.

ADAM. Yes. Adam Quinn. *(They shake hands.)*

EMMA. I'm Emma. Emma Richardson.

PRINCIPAL. Twilight's mom, I presume? *(She shakes EMMA's hand.)*

EMMA. Yes.

PRINCIPAL. Nice to meet you both. Hello, Twilight.

TWILIGHT. Hello, Principal.

PRINCIPAL. Cody.

CODY. Hi, Principal.

PRINCIPAL *(to KIDS)*. Any idea why you're here?

TWILIGHT / CODY. No. / Nope.

PRINCIPAL. I thought as much. *(Looks at PARENTS.)* Do you?

PARENTS. No.

PRINCIPAL. Well, at least you're all on the same page! *(She laughs and sits in the remaining chair.)*

ADAM. Can you tell me how long this is going to be? I have a session with my personal trainer in an hour.

PRINCIPAL. I would strongly advise you to cancel your personal training session, Mr. Quinn. This is a rather urgent meeting regarding your child.

ADAM. I guess I can reschedule. *(He takes out his phone and texts.)*

PRINCIPAL. That would be best. *(She stares at ADAM as he texts.)*

ADAM. Done.

PRINCIPAL. Fantastic. Now, let's begin. Cody. Tell us why you think you're here.

CODY. Is it because of the eggs?

PRINCIPAL. Eggs?

ADAM. What eggs?

CODY. Oh, shoot.

TWILIGHT *(laughs)*. Way to go, Cody. They didn't even know until you told them.

CODY. Wait! I just wondered if you thought maybe the eggs that got thrown in the cafeteria were mine. Which they weren't, by the way. I don't even like eggs.

ADAM. I wondered what happened to our eggs. Why would you do something so stupid, Cody?

PRINCIPAL. That's what we need to ask ourselves, now isn't it? *(To CODY.)* I mean, what did you really gain, Cody? A momentary thrill? Adulation from a few friends who don't have the guts to throw their own eggs at the cafeteria wall? *(TWILIGHT laughs.)* Do you find this amusing, Twilight?

TWILIGHT. No.

PRINCIPAL. I should think not. *(Looks at CODY.)* Tell me, Cody. Do you really think your actions will stop here? Some innocuous broken yolks and egg whites dripping silently down the walls pulling their former protective shell pieces with them as if no one will notice? Don't you realize your thirst for damaging other people's property is just beginning? What's wrong, Cody? Is it your classes? Peer trouble? Perhaps something at home?

ADAM. Wait a minute. Why did home suddenly get mentioned? If Cody did throw eggs at school, he will definitely be reprimanded. But don't assume this is because of something his mother or I did or did not do. We certainly didn't raise our son to throw eggs.

PRINCIPAL *(smiles.)* Few people do. However, we mustn't get defensive while trying to help those we love. After all, I'm sure you've done your best. Not everyone is an exemplary father.

ADAM. Hold on! I'm a very good dad!

PRINCIPAL. Please, Mr. Quinn. I meant in general. Not you, necessarily. Twilight? Any ideas?

TWILIGHT. I think Cody threw the eggs.

CODY. Thanks a lot!

PRINCIPAL. I meant any idea as to why you're here.

TWILIGHT. Oh. Sorry, Cody.

CODY. Whatever.

TWILIGHT. I'm guessing it might have something to do with the locker room?

PRINCIPAL. What happened in the locker room?

TWILIGHT. I heard that someone spray painted some of the lockers. But it wasn't me.

CODY. Yeah, right…

TWILIGHT. I didn't!

PRINCIPAL. I know you didn't, Twilight. I think graffiti is child's play compared to what you've been up to.

EMMA *(to PRINCIPAL)*. I don't like your accusations! I'm sure my daughter will admit to whatever it is she actually did. Why don't you stop beating around the bush by asking our kids what they think they did wrong? I've never heard such nonsense! They either did something or they didn't. If they did, let's address it. If they didn't, stop wasting our time!

ADAM. Amen, sister!

(PRINCIPAL gets up from her chair and begins to walk around as if in a courtroom.)

PRINCIPAL. I can assure you that I have more experience in these matters than you can imagine. While my techniques may be new to you, I have a one hundred percent improvement rate at every school that I've worked for. One hundred percent. I begin by asking for the truth. *(To PARENTS.)* I think you would both agree when I say that our teenage population isn't as forthcoming as they could be.

TWILIGHT. I just want to say that I didn't have anything to do with the recent bullying situation.

EMMA. You better not have, young lady, or else you will be very, very sorry!

PRINCIPAL. Ah, the bullying incident. I'm so glad that you brought that up. Have you ever felt bullied, Twilight?

TWILIGHT. Yeah. A few times.

EMMA. Who? Who has bullied you? I want to know right now!

PRINCIPAL. Please, Mrs. Richardson. *(To TWILIGHT.)* How did it make you feel? To be bullied.

TWILIGHT. Pretty awful.

PRINCIPAL. Of course. But do you really think that by perpetrating those actions onto someone else, you can rid yourself of that pain?

EMMA. What are you inferring? Why don't you just tell us who bullied my daughter?

PRINCIPAL. Mrs. Richardson, I am asking you as kindly as I can. Please stop interrupting me. You are not helping your daughter's case one iota.

EMMA *(stands)*. Case?! Are we in court? Because the last time I checked, we were in a high school. And YOU are supposed to be the one in charge!

PRINCIPAL *(calmly but with intensity and power)*. Indeed. I am the one in charge. I am the one who decides what happens to the children in this establishment. I am the one who will decide what the outcome will be after this meeting. So please, Mrs. Richardson. Sit down or I will call the police.

(Following lines are quick and overlapped.)

EMMA. The police?

ADAM *(to PRINCIPAL)*. What in the world are you talking about?

CODY. Whoa…

TWILIGHT. Mom, chill out!

EMMA *(sits. To PRINCIPAL)*. Fine. But I'm warning you. I have a very good lawyer.

PRINCIPAL. Good to know. *(Smiles and speaks pleasantly.)* Now, if we can get back to why Twilight is here…

TWILIGHT. Okay. I might have said a few mean things to that new girl. She kept talking to my boyfriend, and I told her to stop, but she didn't, so I...I...

PRINCIPAL. You got a group of girls to scare her, correct? Would that be a fair representation of what occurred?

TWILIGHT. Well...

PRINCIPAL. Let me save you a lot of time, Twilight. You may not be aware of this, but per my recommendation, this school installed a very impressive amount of video cameras earlier this year. Including the hallway outside of the girl's locker room.

TWILIGHT. Is that legal?

PRINCIPAL. Oh my, yes. It's commonplace these days. It helps us to monitor the quality of our teachers and of course, keep a watch on our students' safety and behavior. Now is there anything you would like to tell us?

TWILIGHT. Fine. She kept talking to my boyfriend. Even after I told her to stop.

CODY. All she asked him was where her next class was.

TWILIGHT. Shut up, Cody! Were you by the girl's locker room?

CODY. No, but she told me what happened.

TWILIGHT. Whose side are you on, loser?

CODY. Not yours.

ADAM. Don't you call my son a loser!

EMMA. Don't you dare yell at my daughter! You have a lot of nerve for someone who wanted to be with his personal trainer rather than a meeting for his own child!

ADAM. Mind your own business, lady!

(ALL—except PRINCIPAL—begin yelling at one another. They get out of their chairs and right when it seems as if someone might get physical, PRINCIPAL blows a whistle. ALL stop yelling.)

PRINCIPAL. Please. Have a seat.

(They do. They move their chairs farther away from one another.)

PRINCIPAL *(cont'd)*. Please take a look in that corner. *(She points up. They ALL look.)*

CODY. Is that a video camera?

PRINCIPAL. High def. I hear it's the best money can buy!

EMMA. Oh my god.

PRINCIPAL. Well. I think it's safe to say that I can make my decision now. It's all rather clear to tell you the truth. I believe in fair, but effective consequences to one's behavior. My decisions don't always make me the most popular principal, but alas, popularity is for movie stars. I'm simply trying to make the world a better place.

ADAM *(sarcastically)*. We can see that...

PRINCIPAL *(to CODY)*. For your behavior of throwing eggs in the cafeteria and quite a few other places such as the boy's bathrooms, locker rooms, library and study hall...

ADAM *(to CODY)*. You've got to be kidding me!

PRINCIPAL. Your father will spend the remaining year cleaning the school.

ALL. What?

ADAM. Very funny.

PRINCIPAL. Your janitor's uniform is ready for you, and today you will be starting with the boys' bathrooms. Dried egg is surprisingly difficult to remove I hear.

ADAM *(to PRINCIPAL)*. You're insane, lady! I don't know what you think you're doing here, but I'm calling my lawyer! *(He gets his cell phone and begins to dial as:)*

(PRINCIPAL looks at camera and gestures for someone to come in. GUARDS enter and stand on either side of ADAM.)

PRINCIPAL. I would strongly suggest that you go with them, Mr. Quinn.

ADAM *(sarcastically)*. Right.

(GUARDS each take one of ADAM's arms and begin to escort him off.)

ADAM *(cont'd., to GUARDS)*. Get your hands off of me, you— *(Into phone.)* Yes, I need to speak to Ms. Clancy! Hurry! It's an emergency!

(GUARDS take his phone. They drag him off.)

ADAM *(cont'd., as he is taken offstage)*. Let go of me, you idiots! You can't make me do this! I didn't throw the eggs! What is wrong with you?!? Cody, call your mother!

(ALL are in shock.)

PRINCIPAL *(as if nothing has happened)*. Mrs. Richardson. I have always felt strongly that our children learn from their parents first, don't you agree? I mean, the teachers are always being blamed for everything. But let's face it. The parents are doing the most damage. For the remaining year, you will work as the school nurse's assistant.

EMMA. But I don't have any training!

PRINCIPAL. No worries! The school nurse has graciously agreed to teach you everything you'll need to know! You'll help her examine sick kids, clean up their unfortunate vomit, and so forth, and basically learn to be a more compassionate person. I really feel that this will help Twilight to control her bullying behavior, don't you?

EMMA. There is no way that I am going to—

PRINCIPAL. Guards?

(GUARDS enter and begin to escort EMMA off.)

EMMA *(to PRINCIPAL)*. You're out of your mind! Twilight, call my mom and tell her to call the police! *(Exits kicking and yelling.)*

(Silence. TWILIGHT and CODY are terrified.)

PRINCIPAL. Well, I think that about wraps up our meeting! Please help me put these chairs away. Oh, and don't bother calling the police. They've recently hired me to help them cut teen crime in this area. Apparently my methods are really catching on!

CODY. But…what about us?

PRINCIPAL. What about you?

TWILIGHT. What are you going to make us do?

PRINCIPAL. Oh, I think living with your parents for the rest of the year will be plenty, don't you? Grab the chairs! Chop, chop! *(She exits.)*

(TWILIGHT and CODY stare at PRINCIPAL as she exits. They pick up chairs and carry them off as lights fade.)

END

NOTES

NOTES

NOTES

NOTES

NOTES

NOTES